"In Church history God has consistently and persistently urged the Church toward a fulfillment of Jesus' high priestly prayer, that we may be one as he and the Father are one (John 17:21). Fernando Arzola's book is an important contribution to the trialogue among the Orthodox, Catholic and Evangelical Protestant expressions of the Christian faith, helping move the Church toward unity in Kingdom essentials while allowing and even embracing diversity in distinctives and perspectives within these three streams of Christianity. The call to implement ancient practices of the Church in the multiplicity of contemporary contexts is salient. Dr. Arzola's commitment to searching for, understanding, and even experiencing commonalities in the various expressions of the one, common Biblical narrative in Christian worship is a step toward reinforcing the critical unity to which God calls Christians in the one holy catholic and apostolic Church."

## —JAMES R. HART

President
Robert E. Webber Institute for Worship Studies

"In a postmodern era all churches are faced with the need to reach back behind the enlightenment to find theologies, patterns and ceremonies to help them move forward in creative but orthodox worship. This timely study searches out theologies of worship in the classical traditions and makes useful suggestions of how the best can be used in blended worship."

## —BRYAN D. SPINKS

Goddard Professor of Liturgical Studies & Pastoral Theology
Yale Institute of Sacred Music and Yale Divinity School

"A pioneering achievement! This ecumenical study compares and integrates Catholic, Evangelical, and Orthodox teachings on corporate worship. The specific worship practices which the author proposes here can deepen our understanding and experience of worship. Yet at a time when Christianity is rapidly becoming a post-denominational community, Dr. Arzola reminds us that contemporary creativity must grow out of theological continuity with the church's great tradition. Our differences do matter, but there remains a precious core of common faith that can and should unite us all in the worship of the Triune God. This book shows us what that core is and how we might begin to manifest it in our worship practices today."

—**BRADLEY NASSIF**
Professor of Biblical and Theological Studies
North Park University

"In an age of increasing multiculturalism, globalization, ecumenical and inter-religious dialogue, this volume contributes much to discussion about and practice of Catholic, Evangelical and Orthodox worship. The author, a professional religious educator, makes historical perspectives of worship relevant for contemporary life in an attempt to foster deeper understanding and experience of worship. He shows that these three streams of Christianity have much potential to enrich and enhance each other's practice of worship. Written in a clear and cogent style, this work is a gift to religious educators and the people they serve. It should enjoy wide readership and deep discussion."

—**GLORIA DURKA**
Professor and Director of PhD Program in Religious Education
Fordham University

"Fernando Arzola Jr.'s book represents a primer on worship from four perspectives, Catholic, Orthodox, Evangelical, and what he calls a "Historically Orthodox Evangelical" perspective. Sketching each with broad strokes, it performs a useful service in arguing for a recovery of the Church's traditional *lex orandi* or order of worship, while incorporating insights from each tradition."

**—THOMAS P. RAUSCH, SJ**
T. Marie Chilton Professor of Catholic Theology
Loyola Marymount University

"Not only has Arzola shown that there is much that we can learn from Christian worship traditions other than our own, he has also offered a practical way of appropriating the liturgical resources of these traditions. It is especially useful for congregations looking for something more substantial in their Sunday worship."

**—SIMON CHAN**
Earnest Lau Professor of Systematic Theology
Trinity Theological College in Singapore

"Arzola writes from his educational perspective a basic comparative study of the worship streams of Catholic, Evangelical and Orthodox Christian traditions. He insightfully advocates for the recovery of essential worship practices that hold the potential for educational integration with lectionary based catechesis. Following Robert Webber's work, he seeks to revive a sense of wonder and mystery in worship for which many hunger today."

**—ROBERT W. PAZMIÑO**
Valeria Stone Professor of Christian Education
Andover Newton Theological School

# Exploring Worship

# Exploring Worship

*Catholic, Evangelical, and Orthodox Perspectives*

## FERNANDO ARZOLA JR.

WIPF & STOCK · Eugene, Oregon

EXPLORING WORSHIP
Catholic, Evangelical, and Orthodox Perspectives

Wipf & Stock
An Imprint of Wipf and Stock Publishers
199 W. 8th Ave., Suite 3
Eugene, OR 97401
www.wipfandstock.com

ISBN 13: 978-1-61097-092-1

Manufactured in the U.S.A.

# 7126363343

# Contents

# Preface

## THE LAW OF PRAYER DETERMINES
## THE LAW OF BELIEF

Eᴀʀʟʏ ɪɴ the fifth century, Prosper of Aquitaine (c. 390–455 CE) published a manuscript defending the teaching of Augustine of Hippo. In this work, Prosper responds to the claims of the Semi-Pelagians, who believed that a person has the capacity to seek and move toward God on his or her own, apart from the Holy Spirit, with God then completing the salvation process.[1] For Prosper, following Augustine's teaching, salvation begins with, and is completed entirely at, God's initiative.[2] Prosper also claims that *ut legem credendi lex statuat supplicandi*, which is commonly translated "the law of prayer determines the law of belief."[3]

Over the centuries, the terms *lex credendi* and *lex supplicandi* (later *lex orandi*) have become part of the Christian religious lexicon, used in claims about worship and doctrine and the nature of the significant relationship between them. Prosper's assertion about this relationship is clear: how we pray expresses what we believe.

1. De Letter, *Prosper.*
2. Hauck, "Prosper of Aquitaine."
3. De Letter, *Prosper*, 232 n. 1. See also Hohenstein, "Lex Orandi, Lex Credendi." For further study, see Van Slyke, "Lex orandi lex credendi."

## AIM AND OUTLINE

This book examines Catholic, Evangelical, and Orthodox beliefs about and teachings on corporate worship and describes classical practices which can help deepen an understanding and experience of Christian worship. The following clarification of terms may assist the reader:

First, the analysis of Evangelical systematic theology is divided along the lines of two overarching viewpoints, the traditional Evangelical perspective and the historically orthodox Evangelical perspective. In this text, "traditional Evangelicals" will be referred to as such, while representatives of the historically orthodox Evangelical perspective will be called "orthodox Evangelicals."

Second, the terms "Roman Catholic" and "Catholic," and "Roman Catholic Church" and "Catholic Church" are not co-extensive. This study examines the Catholic Church primarily through the Roman Catholic perspective. Thus, the term "Roman Catholic" refers specifically to those who are members of the Church of Rome, whereas the term "Catholic" includes both members of the Roman Catholic Church and those of the Eastern Catholic churches, which are in full communion with Rome.[4]

---

4. When the *Catechism of the Catholic Church* refers to "the Catholic Church" it includes the Roman Catholic Church, which it identifies as "pre-eminent" and those "particular Churches" that are in communion with the Church of Rome. The *Catechism* (paras. 833–834) explains this matter as follows:

> The phrase "particular Church," which is first of all the diocese (or eparchy), refers to a community of the Christian faithful in communion of faith and sacraments with their bishop ordained in apostolic succes-

Third, there is certainly kinship—especially in matters of worship—between the Eastern Catholic churches and the Eastern Orthodox Church, which is not in communion with the Roman Catholic Church. In this book, however, the term "Orthodox Christians" refers specifically to members of the Eastern Orthodox Church and not to members of Eastern Catholic churches. Worship in the Eastern Catholic churches is not treated in this study.

Chapter 1, "Traditional Evangelical Perspectives on Corporate Worship," examines worship from a traditional Evangelical perspective. It focuses on the works of Millard J. Erickson, Stanley J. Grenz, and Wayne A. Grudem. Chapter 2, "Catholic Perspectives on Corporate Worship," examines worship from a Catholic perspective and focuses on the teachings of the *Catechism of the Catholic Church*. Chapter 3, "Orthodox Perspectives on Corporate Worship," examines worship from an Orthodox perspective, focusing on the work of Thomas Hopko, Vladimir Lossky, Alexander Schmemann, and Timothy (Kallistos) Ware.

---

sion. These particular Churches "are constituted after the model of the universal Church; it is in these and formed out of them that the one and unique Catholic Church exists."

Particular Churches are fully catholic through their communion with one of them, the Church of Rome "which presides in charity." "For with this church, by reason of its pre-eminence, the whole Church, that is the faithful everywhere, must necessarily be in accord." Indeed, "from the incarnate Word's descent to us, all Christian churches everywhere have held and hold the great Church that is here [at Rome] to be their only basis and foundation since, according to the Savior's promise, the gates of hell have never prevailed against her."

Chapter 4, "Historically Orthodox Evangelical Perspectives on Worship," examines worship from a historically orthodox Evangelical perspective and focuses on the works of Donald G. Bloesch, Simon Chan, Thomas C. Oden, and Robert E. Webber. Chapter 5, "Re-appropriating Classical Worship Practices," presents six classical worship practices that might be reclaimed for congregational use.

## AUDIENCE AND SIGNIFICANCE

This book was written for those interested in theology, religious education, spiritual formation, and worship/liturgical studies. It is distinctive in at least three ways: First, it engages in a comparative analysis of corporate worship from the perspective of three streams of Christianity—Catholic, Evangelical, and Orthodox. Second, it explores historical perspectives of worship and applies them to the contemporary scene. Finally, this author hopes it will serve as a scholarly reference for those seeking deeper theological reflection on worship, even as it offers practical suggestions for implementing ancient practices that can deepen the understanding and experience of Christian worship.

Furthermore, this study is significant in at least four ways: Theologically, it seeks to contribute to the important and continuing *tri*-alogue between and among Catholics, Evangelicals, and Orthodox. Historically, it highlights the potential for collaboration among these three groups, in contrast to their history of mutual distrust and outright animosity. In relation to spirituality, this work offers a sympathetic examination of worship rooted in the rich history and traditions of the church, an examination that may assist

Christians seeking to deepen their devotional expressions. Pedagogically, the text describes practices that can help deepen the understanding and experience of worship.

A final note: The author is trained in the field of religious education, and he therefore addresses the subject of worship primarily as a Christian religious educator and not as a liturgical theologian.

# Acknowledgments

I AM grateful to Dr. Gloria Durka, my doctoral studies mentor at Fordham University's Graduate School of Religion and Religious Education. The initial thoughts of this work were born during this period under her guidance and encouragement.

I am eternally grateful to Fr. Yakov Ryklin and the St. Mary Magdalen Orthodox Church in New York, NY. Fr. Yakov catechized and Chrismated my wife and me into the Orthodox Church, and this small and faithful community embraced us and nurtured us in the Faith. It also challenged me to expand my theological insights and ecumenical studies to include the Eastern Christian perspectives.

I am grateful to Lorraine Street, my editor. Lorraine provided sage advice and thoughtful edits throughout the publishing process. She also has the rare gift of making suggestions in a gentle manner, ensuring that my ego would not be overly wounded! Thank you, Lorraine, for your professionalism and kindness.

I am overwhelmed and humbled by the words of those who have endorsed this book. Thank you.

To my wife, Jill, for her love and continuous support of my work. For her patience during my long hours, late nights, and early mornings. For tolerating my jokes—which I repeat over and over again! And for journeying with me through this pilgrimage of life. I love you, Jill.

To my daughter, Nicole, who has patiently attended every possible congregation, denomination, and worship tradition throughout the Christian spectrum and has provided me with helpful insight—from store-front churches to Catholic cathedrals, from Spanish-speaking Pentecostal services to Eastern Orthodox liturgies. I love you, Nicole.

# Traditional Evangelical Perspectives on Worship

## UNDERSTANDING EVANGELICAL WORSHIP

WORSHIP MAY be understood as the act of glorifying God, an act performed by a community of faith. For traditional Evangelicals, however, worship is a deeper, all-encompassing life experience.

Stanley J. Grenz, in *Theology for the Community of God*, asserts that worship is the ultimate purpose of the church; indeed, he believes this is why Christ initially instituted it. Grenz writes: "The church in all its expressions exists ultimately for the sake of the glory of the triune God . . . Although God made all creation in order to praise his name, something has gone wrong. In our sinfulness, we fail in our task of living for the divine glory . . . Christ came with this purpose in view . . . Jesus placed his impending sacrifice in the context of glorification: 'Father, the time has come. Glorify your Son, that your Son may glorify you . . . I have brought you glory on earth by completing the work you gave me to do.' (John 17:1b, 4) . . . The fundamental purpose of the church, therefore, is to bring glory to God."[1]

1. Grenz, *Theology*, 487–488.

In his book, *Systematic Theology*, Wayne Grudem develops this notion by explaining the relationship between
worship and glorification: "The term worship is sometimes
applied to all of a Christian's life and it is rightly said that
everything in our life should be an act of worship and everything the church does should be considered worship, for
everything we do should glorify God . . . Worship is the
activity of glorifying God in his presence with our voices
and hearts."[2]

The focus of this chapter is worship within the context
of the gathered faith community. What is the purpose of
worship in the local congregation? According to Grudem,
". . . the primary reason that God called us into the assembly
of the church is that as a corporate assembly we might worship him . . ." Worship is therefore a direct expression of our
ultimate purpose for living: ". . . to glorify God and fully
enjoy him forever."[3]

The community worships God for two reasons. First,
they worship God for who he is: God is the Holy One and
the Creator.[4] Second, they worship him for what he does,
for his saving acts, supremely exemplified by his gift of salvation in Jesus Christ.[5] And, Grenz adds, ". . . the risen Lord
is now the recipient of worship."[6]

Furthermore, the worship of God ". . . reminds us that
God is worthy of worship and we are not."[7] Therefore, the

2. Grudem, *Systematic Theology*, 1003.

3. Grudem, *Systematic Theology*, 1003, 1004.

4. Grenz, *Theology*, 491.

5. Ibid., 491.

6. Ibid., 491.

7. Grudem, *Systematic Theology*, 1004.

overall content and flow of the worship service should point to God and glorify him alone, avoiding, as much as possible, anything that might draw attention to us. According to Grudem, ". . . because God is worthy of worship and seeks to be worshipped, everything in our worship services should be designed and carried out not to call attention to ourselves or bring glory to ourselves, but to call attention to God and to cause people to think about him."[8] Grudem asserts that the worship of God is of great significance and has eternal value: "Because God is eternal and omniscient, the praise that we give him will never fade from his consciousness but will continue to bring delight to his heart for all eternity."[9]

Millard J. Erickson, in his book, *Christian Theology*, describes how worship is distinct from the church's other functions. He also argues that, if worship is collapsed into other tasks, the healthy and growing body of Christ will be damaged. "In worship, the members of the church focus on God; in instruction and fellowship, they focus on themselves and fellow Christians; in evangelism, they turn their attention to non-Christians . . . Worship of God will suffer if the gathering of the body becomes oriented primarily to the interaction among Christians, or if the service is aimed exclusively at evangelizing the unbelievers who are present."[10]

8. Ibid., 1005.
9. Ibid., 1009–1010.
10. Erickson, *Christian Theology*, 1066–1067.

## The Means of Worship

What are the principal activities that serve as vehicles of worship for the traditional Evangelical? Grenz identifies four: (1) music, (2) declaration, (3) prayer, and (4) symbolic act.[11]

For traditional Evangelicals, music is a significant means of worshipping, although preferred styles vary from congregation to congregation. Music sung may range from classic Protestant hymns to charismatic expressions to contemporary Christian music. One specific preference of many traditional Evangelical communities is ". . . songs that address God directly in the second person (that is, speaking to God as 'you' rather than speaking about him as 'he')."[12]

Declaration is just that: declaring or telling one another of the greatness and goodness of God. At the heart of worship is the zenith point of that declaration, i.e., the proclamation of God's Word in the sermon.[13] For traditional Evangelicals, sacred Scripture contains all that is necessary for salvation and all that must be believed. Therefore, worship is normally designed to reach its crescendo with the sermon, which is delivered near the end of the service. Grenz explains: "This practice is correct insofar as it highlights the central role of the Scriptures in community life and the importance of understanding Scripture for community vitality. But implicit in the sermon is also its role as a specific way in which the people of God declare his goodness. As the church gathers to hear the sermon, they are celebrating the divine provision of instruction in the

11. Grenz, *Theology*, 492.

12. Grudem, *Systematic Theology*, 1012.

13. Grenz, *Theology*, 492.

present as an outgrowth of the Spirit's formulation of the Bible in the past."[14] Prayer is an aspect of declaration, in which community members turn their focus away from one another and direct it to God.[15] Grenz suggests the acronym "ACTS" as a way of denoting the four prayer types used in worship: (1) adoration, (2) confession, (3) thanksgiving, and (4) supplication.[16]

The fourth traditional vehicle of worship is symbolic act. Grenz believes the symbolic act is very important; however, he admits that, within Protestantism, it may be the least often used, least important, and least ritualistically significant of the four vehicles, a consequence of the historical discomfort of Protestants with the practices of the medieval church.[17] The central symbolic acts in the life of the church are the ordinances, because they symbolize the gospel, i.e., they re-enact its very heart—"our death and resurrection with Christ."[18] Grenz also suggests that other less important, but still significant symbolic acts—including handshakes, joining hands, and collecting financial gifts—should be considered part of worship.[19]

14. Ibid., 493.
15. Ibid., 494.
16. Ibid., 494–495.
17. Ibid., 495.
18. Ibid., 519–520. This notion will be addressed more fully later in this chapter.
19. Ibid., *Theology*, 495.

## The Results of Worship

While the purpose of worship is to glorify God, traditional Evangelicals believe that blessings flow from genuine worship. Grudem identifies seven such blessings:[20]

The first is that we delight in God. In glorifying God, we enjoy and delight in being in his presence. Second, God delights in us. When we love and praise God, we bring joy and delight to him. This should serve as an encouragement to us. Third, we draw near to God. In the Old Testament, the people of Israel could not enter the temple; they had to remain in the courtyard. Even the high priest could only enter the holy of holies once a year. Under the new covenant, believers can now go directly to the holy of holies: they can worship God directly. Grudem explains this principle, critical to traditional Evangelicals, this way: "This is the reality of new covenant worship: it actually is worship in the presence of God, though we do not see him with our physical eyes, nor do we see the angels gathered around his throne or the spirits of believers who have gone before and are now worshipping in God's presence. But it is all there, and it is all real, more real and more permanent than the physical creation that we see around us, which will someday be destroyed in the final judgment."[21]

Fourth, God draws near to us. In Jas 4:8 we read: "Draw near to God and he will draw near to you" (NRSV). God makes himself known to us in genuine worship. Fifth, God ministers to us. As we worship God, we are edified. "When

20. A more complete description of these results may be found in Grudem, *Systematic Theology*, 1005–1009.

21. Grudem, *Systematic Theology*, 1007.

we worship God, he meets with us and directly ministers to us, strengthening our faith, intensifying our awareness of his presence and granting refreshment to our spirits."[22] Most important, during genuine worship we ". . . experience an intensification of the sanctifying work of the Holy Spirit that is at work continually changing us into the likeness of Christ."[23]

Sixth, the Lord's enemies flee. When the community of faith worships God in Spirit, God strengthens the community and battles the demonic forces that oppose the gospel. The seventh blessing is that unbelievers know they are in God's presence.

## Worship and the Holy Spirit

Worship is a spiritual activity. Ultimately, if it is to be effective it must be empowered by the Holy Spirit.[24] Grudem writes: "We must pray that the Holy Spirit will enable us to worship rightly. The fact that genuine worship is to be carried out in the unseen, spiritual realm is evident in Jesus' words: 'The hour is coming, and now is, when the true worshippers will worship the father in spirit and truth, for such the father seeks to worship him. God is spirit, and those who worship him must worship in spirit and truth.' (John 4:23–24) . . . To worship in 'spirit and truth' is best understood to mean not 'in the Holy Spirit,' but rather 'in the spiritual realm, in the realm of spiritual activity.'"[25]

22. Ibid., 1008.
23. Ibid., 1008.
24. Ibid., 1010.
25. Ibid., 1010.

## SACRAMENTS OR ORDINANCES?

## History of Ordinances

The early, Greek-speaking Christian church used the term *mystērion*, i.e., mystery, to refer to what, in the English-speaking Western church, are now called the sacraments or ordinances.[26] Theologians in the West whose primary language was Latin used the term *sacramentum*, i.e., sacrament, a secular word that referred to ". . . the oath of fidelity and obedience to one's commander sworn by a Roman soldier upon enlistment in the army. Or the term could designate a bond money deposited in a temple pending the settlement of a legal dispute."[27] Latin Christians adopted this word and applied its foundational definitions to their religious observances and sacred objects. Augustine later differentiated between a sacrament itself—i.e., the act itself—and the grace the Spirit imparts through or as a result of this act being performed.[28] This notion in time developed into the classic understanding of a sacrament as ". . . an outward, visible sign of an inward, invisible grace."[29]

Over the centuries, and reaching its peak in the Middle Ages, sacramentalism became linked to sacerdotalism. On the one hand, ". . . a sacrament was a cause of grace in that it

26. Grenz, *Theology*, 512. Note that Eastern churches continue to use the term "holy mysteries." But see *Table and Tradition*, (at p. 55) in which Alasdair Heron claims that ". . . *mysterion* does not refer to sacred rites, but to the hidden things of God disclosed in Christ."

27. Grenz, *Theology*, 513.

28. Ibid., 513.

29. Ibid., 513. See also Kelly, *Early Christian Doctrines*, 422–23.

was God's chosen means of dispensing grace to humans."[30] On the other hand, it was thought that if sacraments were to be efficacious, they needed a consecrated officiator, the priest, who is the instrument of God, and who serves as the channel of divine grace.[31] For his part, Martin Luther agreed that the sacraments infused spiritual vitality; however, he rejected the notion that sacraments infused grace *ex opera operato*, i.e., simply by having been performed. Luther argued that sacramental efficacy requires faith on the part of the participant in the sacramental act.[32] Other Reformers thought Luther did not go far enough. English Baptists, for example, began to replace "sacrament" with "ordinance." The word ordinance is derived from the verb "to ordain": an ordinance therefore ". . . is simply a practice which Christ ordained. Thus, the word designates those special acts the Lord himself instituted."[33]

## Ordinance and Obedience

An emphasis on obedience to the ordinances is a distinct feature of Evangelical theology. As Grenz explains: "Believers participate in the ordinances out of a desire to be obedient to the one who ordained these acts for the church. The ordinances, therefore, are signs of obedience . . . As his obedient disciples, we naturally desire to continue those practices which Christ ordained for us to follow."[34] The theological

30. Grenz, *Theology*, 513.

31. Ibid., 513.

32. Ibid., 514.

33. Ibid., 514.

34. Ibid., 514–515.

significance of this act of obedience is that it understands the ordinance to be fundamentally a human, not a divine, act. Traditional Evangelical theology thus maintains the original meaning of *sacramentum*, i.e., an act of faithful commitment. Grenz writes:

> Rather than God's imparting grace to the communicant through the act, an ordinance provides an occasion for the participant to bear testimony to the spiritual gifts symbolized in it . . . Unless the symbolized spiritual realities are present in the life of the participant, the acts are meaningless . . . Through the sacred practices we affirm our fidelity to our Lord Jesus Christ. These acts provide a significant means for us to confess our faith . . . Through these acts we "act out" our faith. As we affirm our faith in this vivid symbolic manner, the Holy Spirit uses these rites to facilitate our participation in the reality the acts symbolize.[35]

In traditional Evangelical circles, this notion is given popular expression in, for example, the explanation of the need to have conscious faith prior to participating in the ordinance of Baptism. It is said: "Without faith, you go in a dry devil and you come out a wet devil." Despite their standing in traditional Evangelical theology, the ordinances are not widely practiced, although many traditional Evangelicals regret this neglect. Grenz observes:

> It is interesting to note, for example, that many Baptists, whose denominational name derives from the ordinance, often view this act as having

35. Ibid., 514, 516.

no real importance beyond forming the entrance into the local church . . . Recent decades, however, have shown signs that entrenched loyalties to older positions may be giving way to a willingness to learn from a variety of traditions . . . theologians are attempting to develop an alternative to both medieval sacramentalism and the modern rejection of any sacramental understanding. Their endeavor offers a basis for us to reaffirm a sacramental significance for the acts of commitment, while retaining the primacy of the designation "ordinance."[36]

## Number of Ordinances

In 1274, the Council of Lyons affirmed the seven sacraments of the Catholic Church: Baptism, Confirmation, Penance, Eucharist, Holy Orders, Marriage, and the Anointing of the Sick. Several hundred years later, the Reformers rejected five of these, accepting only Baptism and the Lord's Supper. These two sacraments, they argued, are the only ones in which Jesus directly participated. The Anabaptists included a third sacred act: foot-washing, emphasizing true Christian humility and symbolizing the washing of the soul. Few Reformers agreed, however, and foot-washing never received the status of an ordinance in the larger church.[37]

For traditional Evangelicals, a symbolic act should only be elevated to the status of an ordinance if there is biblical evidence that the early church community practiced the act

36. Ibid., 515.
37. Ibid., 519.

in conscious obedience to Christ. Ordinances are symbols of the gospel in that they ". . . reenact the heart of the Gospel, namely, our death and resurrection with Christ."[38] Baptism and The Lord's Supper are accepted as *bona fide* ordinances because the apostolic churches evidently practiced both of them ". . . in a conscious attempt to obey the Lord's intent,"[39] as recounted in Matt 28:19–20; Luke 22:19; Acts 2:41, 8:36, 10:47–48; and 1 Cor 11:17–34. Furthermore, they are accepted because Christ himself participated in them; they are thus understood to be acts his followers should emulate. With respect to the other five sacraments accepted by the Catholic Church, Grenz explains why the Evangelical position differs: ". . . we fail to discover explicit foundation in the corporate life in the New Testament community for treating them as acts of commitment."[40]

The case of foot-washing is interesting, because it arguably meets the tests set out by traditional Evangelicals. It is a symbolic act that Jesus performed, and he explicitly commanded his followers to do likewise, as John 13:12–15 attests: "After he had washed their feet, had put on his robe, and had returned to the table, he said to them, 'Do you know what I have done to you? You call me Teacher and Lord—and you are right, for that is what I am. So if I, your Lord and Teacher, have washed your feet, you also ought to wash one another's feet. For I have set you an example, that you also should do as I have done to you'" (NRSV). Nevertheless, the early church apparently did not view it as a symbolic act that attained the level of an ordinance.

38. Ibid., 519–520.

39. Ibid., 519.

40. Ibid., 519.

## THE LORD'S SUPPER

While Baptism is the initiatory rite, in his *Introduction to Christian Doctrine*, Erickson asserts that the Lord's Supper is the continuing rite of the visible Church.[41] Grudem describes it as a sign of continuing fellowship with Christ.[42] Grenz believes that it constitutes a repeated reaffirmation of what we initially declared in Baptism—namely, our new identity in Christ.[43]

## The Meaning of the Lord's Supper

From a traditional Evangelical perspective, the meaning of the Lord's Supper is rich and diverse for a number of important reasons. First, it was established and ordained by Christ. All three synoptic Gospels and 1 Corinthians refer to it.[44] Second, the Lord's Supper symbolizes the death of Christ: the breaking of the bread and the pouring of the cup symbolize the breaking of Christ's body and the pouring of Christ's blood.[45] Third, Jesus commanded us to repeat the act. Both the Gospel of Luke and 1 Corinthians record his command: ". . . do this in remembrance of me" (Luke 22:19, 1 Cor 11:24 (NKJV)). Fourth, the Lord's Supper is a form of proclamation, interpreted in many different ways. Erickson describes it this way: "The Lord's Supper is at least a representational setting forth of the fact and meaning of

41. Erickson, *Introduction to Christian Doctrine*, 363.

42. Grudem, *Systematic Theology*, 988.

43. Grenz, *Theology*, 531.

44. Erickson, *Christian Theology*, 1117.

45. Grudem, *Systematic Theology*, 989.

Christ's death . . . It is also a proclamation of a future fact; it looks forward to the Lord's second coming. Paul writes, 'For whenever you eat this bread and drink this cup, you proclaim the Lord's death until he comes'" [1 Cor 11:26 (NIV)].[46]

Fifth, the Lord's Supper provides spiritual nourishment to all who partake of it. In this sense, traditional Evangelicals agree that the Lord's Supper is sacramental.[47] Grudem states that just as ". . . ordinary food nourishes our physical bodies, so the bread and wine of the Lord's Supper give nourishment to us . . . [they are] spiritual nourishment and refreshment that Christ is giving to our souls."[48] In addition to participation being an act of obedience, it also contributes to our spiritual growth. Sixth, the Lord's Supper is restricted to followers of Christ. Originally, Jesus celebrated communion only with his disciples. In 1 Cor 11:27–34, Paul tells us about the need for self-examination before the meal. Erickson puts it this way: "One must not only be a believer but a practicing believer to take the elements."[49] Seventh, the Lord's Supper represents the Lord's body and, as such, is a means of uniting all believers. The Lord's Supper is for the body of Christ, the church. Erickson underscores the intended unity of the body of Christ in the ordinance of the Lord's Supper and strongly criticizes those groups that would deny other Christians the opportunity to share in the meal. "For the members of the church to be divided into factions and to despise others who partake with them of the one loaf is an abuse and contradiction of the practice. The

46. Erickson, *Christian Theology*, 1119.
47. Ibid., 1120.
48. Grudem, *Systematic Theology*, 990.
49. Erickson, *Christian Theology*, 1120.

Lord's Supper is an ordinance of the church. It cannot be appropriately practiced by separate individuals in isolation."[50]

Finally, the Lord's Supper serves as an affirmation of faith. Grudem writes that, when partaking of the bread and the cup, the Christian proclaims: "I need you and trust you, Lord Jesus, to forgive my sins and give life and health to my soul, for only by your broken body and shed blood can I be saved."[51]

## The Four Dominant Western Views of the Lord's Supper

Within the Western Christian church, there are effectively four dominant understandings of the Lord's Supper: (1) Catholic, (2) Lutheran, (3) Reformed, and (4) Zwinglian. Briefly (this will be addressed again in Chapter 2), the teaching of Catholic theology is that the bread and wine *are* the physical body and blood of Christ;[52] i.e., in the sacrament ". . . an actual metaphysical change takes place."[53] This understanding is called transubstantiation. Furthermore, the Catholic Church understands the Lord's Supper as a sacrificial act and also believes in sacerdotalism, that only an ordained priest is able to consecrate the bread and wine and therefore to be used by God's grace to change them into the body and blood of Christ.

---

50. Ibid., 1121.

51. Grudem, *Systematic Theology*, 991.

52. Erickson, *Introducing Christian Doctrine*, 365. The emphasis on the word "are" is Erickson's.

53. Ibid., 364.

Luther also believed that Christ is physically present in the bread and wine; however, he denied the metaphysical component of the Catholic Church's teaching. "It is not that the bread and wine become Christ's body and blood, but that we now have the body and blood in addition to the bread and wine."[54] The bread and wine *contain* the physical body and blood.[55] This understanding is called consubstantiation. Luther also rejected the Catholic Church's teaching that each enactment of the Lord's Supper is a sacrificial act. Since Christ died and atoned for sin once and for all, there is no need for repeated sacrifices. Luther likewise dismissed the claims of sacerdotalism. The presence of Christ's body and blood is a result of the power of Christ, he argued, not the power of the priest.[56] What is the benefit of the Lord's Supper, according to the Lutheran view? "By partaking of the sacrament one experiences . . . forgiveness of sin and confirmation of the faith."[57]

The Reformed or Calvinistic view is that Christ is present in the Lord's Supper, not physically, but spiritually. The bread and wine *contain spiritually* the body and blood.[58] Calvin illustrated this notion using the sun: the sun remains in the heavens, yet it warms us. "So the radiance of the Spirit conveys to us the communion of Christ's flesh and blood."[59] In the Reformed view, the notion of eating Christ's physical body and blood is absurd. "True communicants are spiritually nourished as the Holy Spirit brings them into closer

54. Ibid., 364.

55. Ibid., 365. The emphasis on the word "contain" is Erickson's.

56. Ibid., 364–365.

57. Ibid., 364.

58. Ibid., 366. The emphasis on the words "contain spiritually" is Erickson's.

59. Ibid., 365.

connection with the person of Christ."[60] What is the benefit of the Lord's Supper according to the Reformed view? "By taking the elements the participant actually receives anew and continually the vitality of Christ. This benefit should not be thought of as automatic, however. The effect of the sacrament depends in large part upon the faith and receptivity of the participant."[61]

The Zwinglian view is that the Lord's Supper is a commemoration. Because Zwingli emphasized the importance of Christ's death, he saw the Lord's Supper as essentially a commemoration of it. The bread and wine *represent* the body and blood.[62] What is the benefit of the Lord's Supper according to the Zwinglian view? "[T]he value of the sacrament lies simply in receiving by faith the benefits of Christ's death. So the effect of the Lord's Supper is no different in nature from, say, the sermon."[63]

## THE TERM THE "LORD'S SUPPER"

While several other terms—e.g., Eucharist and Communion—are used to describe this event, traditional Evangelicals prefer the term the "Lord's Supper." According to Grenz, ". . . this term anchors our practice in the table fellowship that Jesus shared with his followers . . . The designation the "Lord's Supper" emphasizes the function of this rite as an ordinance, an act of commitment Christ has given for us to follow."[64]

60. Ibid., 365.

61. Ibid., 365.

62. Ibid., 366. The emphasis on the word "represents" is Erickson's.

63. Ibid., 365.

64. Grenz, *Theology*, 536.

## The Presence of Christ

Traditional Evangelicals understand the presence of Christ in the Lord's Supper metaphorically and spiritually. The use of the metaphors—"This is my body; this is my blood," or "I am the bread of life"— is seen as no different from Jesus' use of self-descriptive statements, e.g., "I am the way, the truth, and the life," or "I am the vine," or "I am the good shepherd." Traditional Evangelicals therefore tend to ". . . render Jesus' statement this way: 'This represents [or signifies] my body,' and 'This represents [or signifies] my blood.'"[65]

Jesus promises to be with his disciples everywhere and through all time, and further promises that ". . . where two or three are gathered in my name, I am there among them" (Matt 18:20 (NRSV)). Therefore, Jesus is spiritually present in the Lord's Supper. Grudem puts it this way: "Christ is . . . spiritually present in a special way as we partake of the bread and wine."[66] Erickson affirms this notion when he writes that ". . . Christ's special presence in the sacrament is influential rather than metaphysical in nature."[67]

The traditional Evangelical approaches the Lord's Supper as an encounter with Christ, ". . . a time of relationship and communion with Christ, for he has promised to meet with us . . . The Lord's Supper . . . is a time when we are drawn close to Christ, and thus come to know him better and love him more."[68]

65. Erickson, *Christian Theology*, 1130.
66. Grudem, *Systematic Theology*, 995.
67. Erickson, *Christian Theology*, 1130.
68. Ibid., 1131

## The Efficacy of the Lord's Supper

In 1 Cor 11:27–32, Paul writes that some who participated in the Lord's Supper became ill, weak, and even died. The traditional Evangelical understands Paul's explanation of this phenomenon as suggesting that ". . . the effect of the Lord's Supper must be dependent on or proportional to the faith of the believer and his or her response to what is being presented in the rite."[69] Erickson writes: "The Lord's Supper is a reminder of the death of Christ and its sacrificial and propitiatory character as an offering to the Father on our behalf. It further points forward to his second coming. In addition, it symbolizes the unity of believers."[70]

## The Proper Administrator

Who should lead the Lord's Supper? It is proper and in good order that those chosen and empowered by the church to conduct it should do so. In general, those who lead (elder, presbyter, or bishop) and those who assist (deacon) should meet the criteria outlined in 1 Tim 3.

## The Appropriate Recipients

Who should participate in the Lord's Supper? Grudem suggests three criteria. First, since the Lord's Supper signifies a spiritual relationship between a believer and Christ, only genuine believers in Christ should be recipients of the elements.[71] Others may be present, however, during the cel-

69. Ibid., 1131.
70. Ibid., 1131.
71. Grudem, *Systematic Theology*, 996.

ebration of this ordinance. While the Lord's Supper is for believers, according to Grenz ". . . the Spirit can issue a call to any present who are not yet believers. As they see the enactment of the Lord's sacrifice and renewal of the covenant with the Lord believers thereby make, the Spirit calls them to come to Christ in faith and receive the salvation available through him."[72]

Second, ordinarily only those who have been baptized should participate in the Lord's Supper. However, traditional Evangelicals also believe that someone who has not yet been baptized may nevertheless be a genuine believer. While it is not necessarily the desirable or appropriate order for attaining membership in the church, this position nevertheless reaffirms two essential assumptions: (1) that Baptism is not salvific, and (2) that one should have conscious faith if one is to participate in the ordinances.[73]

Finally, the person participating in the Lord's Supper should examine him or herself. In keeping with 1 Cor 11, recipients should not be engaged in flagrant sin. In conducting a self- examination, a person reflects on whether he or she is ". . . acting in ways that vividly portray not the unity of the one bread and one body, but disunity . . . We ought to ask ourselves whether our relationships in the Body of Christ are in fact reflecting the character of the Lord whom we meet there and whom we represent."[74] While the Bible sets out no minimum age for participation in the Lord's Supper, traditional Evangelicals believe communicants should be mature enough to understand its meaning.

72. Grenz, *Theology*, 540–541.

73. Grudem, *Systematic Theology*, 996.

74. Ibid., 997; See also Erickson, *Christian Theology*, 1132.

## THE ELEMENTS OF THE LORD'S SUPPER

Must unleavened bread and wine be used for the Lord's Supper? For traditional Evangelicals, the chief concern is not duplication of the traditional Passover meal; their chief concern is representation and symbolism. Therefore, bread and grape juice are considered both sufficient and appropriate. Erickson explains: "What we are commemorating in the Lord's Supper is not the precise circumstances of its initiation, but what it represented to Jesus and the disciples in the upper room. That being the case, suitability to convey the meaning, not similarity to the original circumstances, is what is important as far as the elements are concerned."[75]

## THE FREQUENCY OF CELEBRATING THE LORD'S SUPPER

Should the Lord's Supper be celebrated daily, weekly, or monthly? There is no clear biblical answer to this question. However, Erickson argues that it should ". . . be observed often enough to prevent long gaps between times of reflection on the truths it signifies, but not so frequently as to make it seem trivial or so commonplace that we go through the motions without really thinking about the meaning."[76]

75. Erickson, *Christian Theology*, 1133.
76. Ibid., 1134.

## 2

# Catholic Church Perspectives on Worship

## FROM WORSHIP TO LITURGY

CATHOLIC TEACHING presents the worship of God as the foundational act of religion. The *Catechism of the Catholic Church* (henceforth *CCC*) declares it explicitly: "Adoration is the first act of the virtue of religion. To adore God is to acknowledge him as God, as the Creator and Savior, the Lord and Master of everything that exists, as infinite and merciful Love."[1] Just as it reminds traditional Evangelicals, the worship of God also reminds Catholics that humans are not the focus of worship. Furthermore, Catholic teaching is that in acknowledging God as the recipient of our worship, we are liberated from self-idolatry. "To adore God is to acknowledge, in respect and absolute submission, the nothingness of the creature who would not exist but for God. . . . The worship of the one God sets man free from turning in on himself, from the slavery of sin and the idolatry of the world."[2]

Catholic theology also refers to the celebration of the gathering faith community as "liturgy," from the Greek

1. *Catechism*, para. 2096.

2. Ibid., para. 2097.

22

word *leitourgia,* which meant "public work" or "service in the name of or on behalf of the people." Liturgy, therefore, is the ". . . participation of the People of God in the work of God."[3] Furthermore, worship is only one aspect of liturgy. The *CCC* states that ". . . in the New Testament, the word "liturgy" refers not only to the celebration of divine worship but also to the proclamation of the Gospel and to active charity . . . In a liturgical celebration the Church is servant in the image of her Lord, the one *leitourgos;* she shares in Christ's priesthood (worship), which is both prophetic (proclamation) and kingly (service of charity)."[4]

## UNDERSTANDING CATHOLIC LITURGY

Catholic theology holds that liturgy is the most sacred action of the Church: it is the action that surpasses all others. "No other action of the Church can equal its efficacy by the same title and to the same degree . . . In the liturgy, all Christian prayer finds its source and goal . . . The liturgy is the summit toward which the activity of the Church is directed; it is also the font from which all her power flows."[5] Catholic theology holds that the liturgy has two dimensions. First, the Church gathers to adore and bless the Father. Second, it seeks from him the divine blessing by pouring out the Holy Spirit. "In the Church's liturgy the divine blessing is fully revealed and communicated."[6]

---

3. Ibid., para. 1069.
4. Ibid., para. 1070.
5. Ibid., paras. 1070, 1073–1074.
6. Ibid., paras. 1082–1083.

Traditional Evangelical worship is undertaken primarily so that the community may glorify God in Christ and hear God's Word. Catholic liturgy is understood differently. It certainly seeks to glorify God in Christ; however, the liturgical action is understood as an ". . . encounter between Christ and the Church."[7] The zenith of this encounter is manifested especially in the sacrament of Holy Communion. When partaking of Holy Communion, one not only receives Christ; the grace of this sacrament helps transform one to be more like Christ. About this effect, the *CCC* states: "The Spirit heals and transforms those who receive him by conforming them to the Son of God. The fruit of the sacramental life is that the Spirit of adoption makes the faithful partakers in the divine nature by uniting them in a living union with the only Son, the Savior."[8]

## FROM ORDINANCE TO SACRAMENT

Catholic theology does not use the term ordinance; rather it speaks of sacrament. The word ordinance implies that these are symbolic acts that *we* do in response to Jesus' commands. A sacrament, by contrast, is understood to be an action that is a sign of grace that *Christ* "does" and confers upon us. According to the *CCC*:

> Sacraments are efficacious signs of grace, instituted by Christ and entrusted to the Church, by which divine life is dispensed to us. The visible rites by which the sacraments are celebrated signify and make present the graces proper to

7. Ibid., para. 1097.
8. Ibid., para. 1130.

each sacrament . . . They are efficacious because in them Christ himself is at work: it is he who baptizes, he who acts in his sacrament in order to communicate the grace that each sacrament signifies . . . Sacraments are powers that come forth from the Body of Christ, which is ever-living and life-giving. They are actions of the Holy Spirit at work in his Body, the Church. Sacramental grace is the grace of the Holy Spirit, given by Christ and proper to each sacrament.[9]

The purpose of the sacraments is ". . . to sanctify men, to build up the Body of Christ and . . . to give worship to God."[10] The sacraments are considered to be sacraments of Christ, sacraments of the Church, sacraments of faith, sacraments of salvation, and sacraments of eternal life.[11] Sacraments ". . . not only presuppose faith, but by words and objects they also nourish, strengthen and express it."[12] They call to memory the words and action of Jesus' life, death, and resurrection, the paschal mystery. They also prefigure the mystery of the heavenly banquet and the future glory.[13]

Sacraments are actions performed both *by* the church and *for* the church. They are performed *by* the Church because the Church is the body of Christ, and they are actions that flow from its mission. Sacraments are also performed *for* the church, for they empower the Church and express its great communion with God.[14]

---

9. Ibid., paras. 1131, 1127, 1116.

10. Ibid., para. 1123.

11. Ibid., paras. 1114–1130.

12. Ibid., para. 1123.

13. Ibid., paras. 1115, 1130.

14. Ibid., para. 1118.

## The Celebrants of the Liturgy

Catholic theology teaches that the liturgy is an action of the whole Christ (*Christus totus*). This includes those who celebrate in the heavenly liturgy as described in the Book of Revelation.[15] In the earthly realm, it is the whole community that celebrates, united with the Christ. More specifically, it is ". . . the community of the baptized who by regeneration and the anointing of the Holy Spirit are consecrated to be a spiritual house and a holy priesthood."[16] The priesthood of the baptized denotes the participation of believers in the vocation of Christ as priest, prophet, and king. All who are baptized share in this "holy priesthood," exercised by the ". . . unfolding of the baptismal grace."[17]

The ministerial priesthood includes, more specifically, those ordained to lead the Church. According to Catholic teaching, through them the presence of Christ is made visible. According to the *CCC*, "[t]hrough the ordained ministry, that of bishops and priests, the presence of Christ as head of the Church is made visible in the midst of the community of believers . . . This presence . . . is not to be understood as if [they] were preserved from all human weaknesses, the spirit of domination, error, even sin. . . . [However], this guarantee [of the power of the Holy Spirit] extends to the sacraments, so that even the minister's sin cannot impede the fruit of grace."[18]

---

15. Ibid., paras. 1136–1137.
16. Ibid., paras. 1140–1141.
17. Ibid., paras. 1546–1547.
18. Ibid., paras. 1549–1550.

## The Means of the Sacraments

Catholics and traditional Evangelicals celebrate the liturgy through a number of common vehicles. For example, singing and music are important components of Catholic liturgies, as they are of the worship services of traditional Evangelicals. The Catholic Church has a long history of praising God through solemn music. More significant still is God's Word, critical to both. The CCC underlines the place of God's Word in the liturgy this way: "The liturgical word and action are inseparable both insofar as they are signs and instruction and insofar as they accomplish what they signify. When the Holy Spirit awakens faith, he not only gives an understanding of the Word of God, but through the sacraments also makes present the wonders of God that it proclaims."[19] Unlike traditional Evangelicals, however, Catholics also use sacred images and icons in worship. They are used to help believers glorify God, as they express, in images, the gospel message. These images of the sacred are intended to awaken and nourish the faith of worshippers.[20]

## THE HOLY EUCHARIST

### The Term "Holy Eucharist"

As the writing of Erickson, Grenz, and Grudem attest, traditional Evangelicals prefer the term "the Lord's Supper" to the term "Eucharist." Catholic theology, affirming the richness of this sacrament, gives it many names: "the Lord's

19. Ibid., para. 1155.
20. Ibid., paras. 1159–1162, 1192.

Supper," "the Breaking of the Bread," "the Eucharistic Assembly," "the Memorial," "the Holy Sacrifice," and "the Holy and Divine Liturgy."[21] "Holy Communion" is also a popular name, ". . . because by this sacrament we unite ourselves to Christ, who makes us sharers in his Body and Blood to form one body."[22] The term "the Holy Mass" is also commonly used ". . . because the liturgy in which the mystery of salvation is accomplished concludes with the sending forth *(missio)* of the faithful."[23] The *CCC*, however, seems to prefer and overwhelmingly uses the term the "Eucharist" when referring to the sacrament of bread and wine, ". . . because it is an action of thanksgiving to God (Eucharist, from the Greek *eucharisteō*, to give thanks)."[24]

## The Relationship between Liturgy and the Eucharist

Catholics view the Eucharist as a constitutive element of the liturgy; that is, the Eucharist is intrinsically linked with the liturgy. More than this, the Holy Eucharist is the ". . . source and summit of the Christian life."[25] Receiving the Eucharist is the ultimate encounter with Christ. "The other sacraments, and indeed all ecclesiastical ministries and works of the apostolate, are bound up with the Eucharist and are oriented toward it. For in the blessed Eucharist is contained the whole spiritual good of the Church, namely Christ himself, our Pasch. . . . It is the culmination both of God's action sanctify-

---

21. Ibid. paras. 1328–1332.
22. Ibid., para. 1331.
23. Ibid., para. 1332.
24. Ibid., para. 1328.
25. Ibid., para. 1324.

ing the world in Christ and of the worship men offer to Christ and through him to the Father in the Holy Spirit . . . In brief, the Eucharist is the sum and summary of our faith: 'Our way of thinking is attuned to the Eucharist and the Eucharist in turn confirms our way of thinking.'"[26]

## The Body and Blood of Christ

According to Catholic theology, the consecration leads to a transubstantiation of the bread and wine: that is, in the consecrated bread and wine ". . . Christ himself, living and glorious, is present in a true, real and substantial manner: his Body and his Blood, with his soul and his divinity."[27] This understanding flows from a soteriological and eschatological reading of John 6:47–58 (NRSV):

> "Very truly, I tell you, whoever believes has eternal life. I am the bread of life. Your ancestors ate the manna in the wilderness, and they died. This is the bread that comes down from heaven, so that one may eat of it and not die. I am the living bread that came down from heaven. Whoever eats of this bread will live for ever; and the bread that I will give for the life of the world is my flesh." The Jews then disputed among themselves, saying, "How can this man give us his flesh to eat?" So Jesus said to them, "Very truly, I tell you, unless you eat the flesh of the Son of Man and drink his blood, you have no life in you. Those who eat my flesh and drink my blood have eternal life, and I will raise them up on the last day; for my flesh is true food and my

26. Ibid., paras. 1324–1325, 1327.

27. Ibid., para. 1413.

blood is true drink. Those who eat my flesh and drink my blood abide in me, and I in them. Just as the living Father sent me, and I live because of the Father, so whoever eats me will live because of me. This is the bread that came down from heaven, not like that which your ancestors ate, and they died. But the one who eats this bread will live for ever."

## The Eucharistic Sacrifice

The memorial of the Eucharistic sacrifice has three facets: First, the Eucharist is a sacrifice of praise and thanksgiving for the work of creation. "In the Eucharistic sacrifice the whole of creation loved by God is presented to the Father through the death and the resurrection of Christ."[28] Second, the Eucharist is the sacrificial memorial of Christ. "The Eucharist is the memorial of Christ's Passover, the making present and the sacramental offering of his unique sacrifice in the liturgy of the Church which is his Body."[29] In the Eucharistic Prayers, this is called the *anamnesis* or memorial.[30] Finally, in this "most blessed sacrament," the presence of Christ in the Eucharist is real and substantial, as the *CCC* explains: ". . . the whole Christ is truly, really, and substantially contained . . . It is by the conversion of the bread and wine into Christ's body and blood that Christ becomes present in this sacrament . . . The Eucharistic presence of Christ begins at the moment of the consecration and endures as long as the Eucharist species subsist . . . In his Eucharistic presence he remains mysteriously in our midst

28. Ibid., paras. 1359–1361.

29. Ibid., paras. 1362–1372.

30. Ibid., para. 1362.

as the one who loved us and gave himself up for us . . . This change the holy Catholic Church has fittingly and properly called transubstantiation."[31] In the liturgy, the altar therefore serves as both an altar of the sacrifice and the table of the Lord.[32]

## THE FRUIT OF HOLY COMMUNION

The *CCC* identifies five benefits of receiving Holy Communion. First, Holy Communion unites us, intimately, with Christ. Second, Holy Communion separates us from sin. "For this reason the Eucharist cannot unite us to Christ without at the same time cleansing us from past sins and preserving us from future sins."[33] Third, through Holy Communion Christ unites us all into one body. Fourth, it commits us to the poor. "To receive in truth the Body and Blood of Christ given up for us, we must recognize Christ in the poorest."[34] Fifth, Holy Communion reinforces the desire of the faithful for the unity of the Church. Standing in the way of that unity, however, is the belief that, as the *CCC* puts it, ". . . ecclesial communities derived from the Reformation and separated from the Catholic Church have not preserved the proper reality of the Eucharistic mystery in its fullness, especially because of the absence of the sacrament of Holy Orders. It is for this reason that, for the Catholic Church, Eucharistic intercommunion with these communities is not possible."[35]

31. Ibid., paras. 1373–1381.
32. Ibid., para. 1383.
33. Ibid., para. 1393.
34. Ibid., para. 1397.
35. Ibid., paras. 1398–1401.

## The Two Parts of the Liturgy

The Catholic liturgy is divided into two principal parts: The Liturgy of the Word and the Liturgy of the Eucharist. Together, they form one single act of worship.[36] The Liturgy of the Word focuses on proclaiming the Word of God, while the Liturgy of the Eucharist is the celebration of the Lord's Supper.

| The Order of Catholic Liturgy | | | |
|---|---|---|---|
| Liturgy of the Word | | Liturgy of the Eucharist | |
| Gathering | Word | Eucharist | Dismissal |
| | Old Testament Psalm New Testament Epistle Gospel Homily/ Sermon Intercessions | Presentation of Bread and Wine Collection/ Offerings Eucharistic Prayers The Lord's Prayer Sign/Exchange of Peace Communion | |

## The Liturgical Year

Like an increasing number of Protestant denominations, the Catholic Church follows an annual cycle called the liturgical or church year, which begins with the First Sunday of Advent. As the church year progresses, so unfolds the ". . . whole mystery of Christ from his Incarnation and Nativity through his Ascension, to Pentecost and the expectation of the blessed

36. Ibid., para. 1346.

hope of the coming of the Lord."[37] Easter Sunday is considered the "Great Sunday," the "Feast of feasts," the "Solemnity of solemnities," and the "Sacrament of sacraments."[38]

## The Liturgical Year

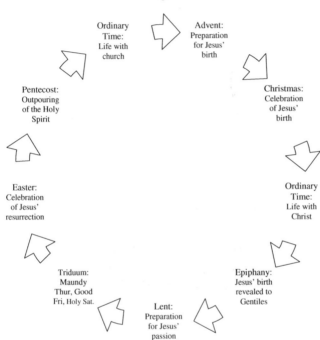

## The Lectionary

The readings for the liturgy are identified in the lectionary, the official book setting out the order of scripture readings for the liturgical year. The lectionary is set up in three, one-

37. Ibid., para. 1194.
38. Ibid., para. 1169.

year cycles simply identified as Cycle A, Cycle B, and Cycle C. Cycle A focuses on the Gospel of Matthew; Cycle B on the Gospel of Mark; Cycle C on the Gospel of Luke. The Gospel of John is used throughout all three cycles.

| THE LECTIONARY | | | |
|---|---|---|---|
| Cycle Starting on the first Sunday of Advent | Cycle A | Cycle B | Cycle C |
| Gospel Focus | Gospel of Matthew | Gospel of Mark | Gospel of Luke |
| | John—used primarily in Lent | John—used primarily in Lent | John—used primarily in Lent |

In addition to the annual cycle, there is a daily cycle of prayer called the "Liturgy of the Hours." The Liturgy of the Hours is a form of public prayer, scheduled at specific times throughout the day. "The celebration of the Liturgy of the Hours demands not only harmonizing the voice with the praying heart, but also a deeper 'understanding of the liturgy and of the Bible, especially the Psalms.'"[39]

---

39. Ibid., paras. 1174–1178.

# 3

# Orthodox Church Perspectives on Worship

## THE DIVINE LITURGY: HEAVEN ON EARTH

IN A.D. 987, Prince Vladimir of Kiev was seeking a religion. He sent a delegation to the Hagia Sophia in Constantinople to attend the liturgy, ". . . so that the Russes might behold the glory of the God of the Greeks."[1] On returning home, his envoys described what they had observed in the following words: "We knew not whether we were in heaven or on earth. For on earth there is no such splendor or such beauty, and we are at a loss how to describe it. We know only that God dwells there among men, and their service is fairer than the ceremonies of other nations. For we cannot forget their beauty."[2]

This story illustrates the Orthodox understanding that in liturgy—the "Divine Liturgy"—one encounters God immediately and directly and experiences the awesome and profound reality of his presence and Kingdom. In *Orthodox Theology and Religious Education*, Constance J. Tarasar states: "In the dimension of worship, we are confronted with a vision and a manifestation—a revelation of who God

1. Taft, *The Byzantine Rite*, 17.
2. Ibid., 18.

is, what he has done for us, and how we are expected to respond to his love."[3]

As the Orthodox understand it, the liturgy effects a union between the human and the divine: a "vertical" union in that heaven comes down to earth, lifting us closer to the Kingdom of God.[4] The Divine Liturgy is the center of Orthodox Christian life. It is the fundamental, central action of the Orthodox Church formally gathered as the people of God.[5] In *The Orthodox Church*, Timothy (Bishop Kallistos) Ware writes: "Orthodoxy sees human beings above all else as liturgical creatures who are most truly themselves when they glorify God and who find their perfection and self-fulfillment in worship."[6] For Orthodox Christians, the Divine Liturgy is not simply a worship service. It is the sacramental manifestation of the church as the community of God in heaven and on earth. Ware explains: "Worship for the Orthodox Church is nothing else than 'heaven on earth.' The holy liturgy is something that embraces two worlds at once, for both in heaven and on earth the liturgy is one and the same—one altar, one sacrifice, one presence . . . in every

3. Tarasar, "Orthodox Theology and Religious Education," 109.

4. In the Eastern tradition, it is sometimes said that during worship, "God condescends and we ascend to heaven." That "God condescends" is not meant derogatorily. It is an Eastern concept expressing the belief that God so loves His creation that He voluntarily leaves his heavenly throne and comes to meet his children as they worship. The idea of "condescending" is most profoundly actualized in the incarnation of Jesus Christ. During liturgy, this "divine union" is most completely actualized in participation in the Holy Eucharist.

5. The word *liturgy is* here understood as *common work* or *common action*.

6. Ware, *The Orthodox Church*, 266.

place of worship . . . not merely the local congregation is present, but the church universal—the saints, the angels, the Mother of God and Christ himself."[7]

This notion is crucial to an understanding of Orthodox worship. Orthodox Christians do not enter worship hoping to be moved by music—whether by classic hymns, Gospel music, or contemporary praise and worship songs. During Orthodox liturgy, prayers and scripture readings are chanted, and the voice is the only instrument used. Furthermore, Orthodox Christians do not come to hear emotionally charged sermons expressing ideas of contemporary relevance. Instead, through the message of the Holy Bible, the stories of the saints, and the teaching of church tradition, Orthodox homilies invite people to move toward "deification," the process by which a Christian becomes more like God. "His divine power has given us everything we need for life and godliness . . . you may participate in the divine nature and escape the corruption in the world caused by evil desires" (2 Pet 1:3–4 (NIV)).

Deification does not, however, mean that humans become divine. We do not become like God in his nature. Orthodox Christians would view such an idea as heresy. The Orthodox notion of deification is actually similar to the Evangelical concept of sanctification. As is explained in the *Orthodox Study Bible*:

> Deification means we are to become more like God through His grace or divine energies. In creation, we were made in the image and likeness of God (Gen 1:26) according to human nature. In other words, humanity by nature is an

7. Ware, "The Earthly Heaven," 12.

icon or image of deity: The divine image is in all humanity. Through sin, however, this image and likeness of God was marred and we fell. When the Son of God assumed our humanity in the womb of the blessed Virgin Mary, the process of our being renewed in God's image and likeness was begun. Thus, those who are joined to Christ through faith, in Holy Baptism begin a process of re-creation, being renewed in God's image and likeness.[8]

## "GOD IS NOT . . .": APOPHATIC THEOLOGY

Eastern Christian theology is rooted in what is called the "apophatic tradition." Apophatism (from the Greek *apophanai*, "to say no") is the concept of "unknowing," as it were; theologically speaking it is an assertion about the inability to fully know God. In his book, *Byzantine Theology*, John Meyendorff explains: "Rejecting . . . the view that the human mind can reach the very essence of God, (the Fathers) affirm the absolute transcendence of God and exclude any possibility of identifying Him with any human concept. By saying what God is not, the theologian is really speaking the Truth, for no human word or thought is capable of knowing what God is."[9]

This concept is significantly different from the position taken by Western Christianity, certainly since the Enlightenment, and particularly by Catholic and Evangelical theology, which is committed to the effort to rationalize, define, and codify God. In *Eastern Orthodox Christianity:*

8. "Deification," *The Orthodox Study Bible*, 1692.
9. John Meyendorff, *Byzantine Theology*, 11–12.

*A Western Perspective*, Daniel B. Clendenin explains: "The West has enthroned reason and logic as the final arbiter of all matters of truth, so much so that is not uncommon for scholars to speak of the autocracy of reason in Western culture. In the West, all truth claims must pass the test of rational intelligibility that is administered at the bar of reason . . . Our theology in the West is not immune from this epistemological orientation; an identifiable tradition in Western theology enshrines human rationality as the decisive criterion of theological truth."[10]

Clendenin's observation is affirmed in the writings of Norman Geisler, a well-respected contemporary Evangelical apologist, who states: "[T]he law of noncontradiction is inviolable; it must 'reign sovereignly and universally over all thinking and speaking about God . . . Human logic controls all our thoughts about reality all the time or we are left with some thoughts and statements about reality that are contradictory.'"[11]

To this philosophical assumption, Vladimir Lossky responds in *The Mystical Theology of the Eastern Church*: "There is no philosophy *more* or *less* Christian. Plato is not more Christian than Aristotle. The question of the relation between theology and philosophy has never arisen in the East. The apophatic attitude gave to the Fathers of the Church that freedom and liberality with which they employed philosophical terms without running the risk of being misunderstood or of falling into a 'theology of concepts.'"[12] While not rejecting reason, Eastern thinkers ". . . do reject what they see as the hubris of reason that

10. Daniel B. Clendenin, *Eastern Orthodox Christianity*, 48, 50.

11. Geisler, "Avoid All Contradictions," 159, 155.

12. Lossky, *Mystical Theology*, 42.

now typifies Western culture. They resist any tendency that would allow or encourage reason to expunge theological mystery and appoint itself as the only criterion of truth."[13] In his book, *Orthodox Theology*, Vladimir Lossky writes eloquently that ". . . God is not the object of a science, and theology differs radically from the thought of philosophers. The theologian does not search for God as man seeks an object; he is seized by Him as one is seized by a person."[14]

According to the Eastern theological perspective, therefore, there are two ways of knowing God: the negative (apophatic) way and the positive (cataphatic) way. Lossky explains: "The negative way attempts to know God not in what He is but in what he is not . . . Thus, side by side with the negative way, the positive way opens out. God Who is the hidden God, beyond all that reveals Him, is also He that reveals Himself. He is wisdom, love, goodness. But His nature remains unknowable in its depths, and that is exactly why He reveals Himself."[15] Of course, the fullness of God's revelation is found in Jesus Christ.

Western thinkers tend to favor a singularly positive (cataphatic) approach to the theological enterprise. The popular Western maxim, that theology is "faith seeking understanding," implies an attempt to rationalize supernatural mystery. Regarding this positive approach, Lossky argues that it ". . . transposes revelation onto the plane of philosophy."[16] On the other hand, in the negative ". . . ap-

13. Clendenin, *Eastern Orthodox Christianity*, 52.

14. Lossky, *Orthodox Theology*, 27.

15. Ibid., 32–33.

16. Vladimir Lossky, "The Procession of the Holy Spirit in Orthodox Trinitarian Theology," 170.

proach, understanding seeks the realities of faith, in order to be transformed by becoming more and more open
to the mysteries of revelation."[17] He continues: "Negative
theology is not merely a theory of ecstasy. It is an expression of that fundamental attitude which transforms the
whole of theology into a contemplation of the mysteries
of revelation. It is not a branch of theology, a chapter, or
an inevitable introduction on the incomprehensibility of
God from which one passes unruffled to a doctrinal exposition in the usual terminology of human reason and
philosophy in general . . . For Christianity is not a philosophical school for speculating about abstract concepts,
but is essentially a communion with the living God."[18] By
acknowledging that God cannot be known, one is left with
room for mystery. Meyendorff writes:

> Eastern Christian theology has often been called
> "mystical." The term is truly correct, provided
> one remember that in Byzantium "mystical"
> knowledge does not imply emotional individu-
> alism, but quite the opposite: a continuous com-
> munion with the Spirit who dwells in the whole
> Church. It implies as well the constant recogni-
> tion of the inadequacies of the human intellect
> and of human language to express the fullness
> of truth, and the constant balancing of positive
> theological affirmations about God with the
> corrective apophatic theology. Finally, it presup-
> poses an "I–Thou" relationship with God, i.e.,
> not knowledge only, but love.[19]

17. Ibid., 170.
18. Lossky, *The Mystical Theology of the Eastern Church*, 42.
19. Meyendorff, *Byzantine Theology*, 14.

For the Orthodox Christian therefore, theological issues such as the transformation of the Eucharist are simply left as mystery. The debates about transubstantiation versus consubstantiation versus memorial symbolism are of no significance to them. How the bread and wine becomes the body and blood of Christ is simply unknown.

## ORTHODOX ARCHITECTURE
## AND SPIRITUAL FORMATION

For the Orthodox Christian, the church building and its aesthetic environment play a significant role in spiritual formation. For the early church, the temple was subordinate to the liturgy, primarily because Christians who publically expressed their faith were ruthlessly oppressed and persecuted. However, the expression of Christian worship was understood through Eucharistic ecclesiology. In his book, *Introduction to Liturgical Theology*, Alexander Schmemann writes: "In the center of the faith and consciousness of the early Christian community there was the experience of the Church as the reality of a living temple, actualized in the Eucharistic assembly."[20] On the night before he died, Jesus partakes of the Last Supper and proclaims to his disciples: "I have eagerly desired to eat this Passover with you before I suffer. For I tell you, I will not eat it again until it finds fulfillment in the kingdom of God" (Luke 22:15–16 (NIV)). The urgency of the early Eucharistic gatherings would surely have made Christ's words even more sobering as believers recognized that martyrdom was likely imminent:

20.  Schmemann, *Introduction to Liturgical Theology*, 114.

the eschatological dimension of the Eucharist would have been immediately apparent.

Over time, however, things changed. Schmemann claims that, ultimately, ". . . the center of attention was shifted from the Church assembled and realized within it to the church building itself, as in fact a sanctified building or sanctuary . . . This was a church-sanctuary, a place for the habitation and residence of the sacred, capable therefore of sanctifying and communicating the sacred to whoever entered it."[21]

## Orthodox Church Architecture—General

Orthodox church architecture is patterned after the image of God's Kingdom suggested by the *Book of Revelation*. It is characterized ". . . by the attempt to reveal the fundamental experience of Orthodox Christianity: God is with us."[22] In *The Orthodox Faith: Worship*, Thomas Hopko writes that Orthodox architecture ". . . reveals that God is with men, dwelling in them and living in them through Christ and Spirit. It does so by using the dome or the vaulted ceiling to crown the Christian church building, the house of the Church which is the people of God. Unlike the pointed arches which point to God far up in the heavens, the dome or the spacious, all-embracing ceiling give the impression that the Kingdom of God, and in the Church, Christ, ". . . unites all things in himself, things in heaven and things on earth" (Eph 1:10).[23]

21. Ibid., 114–115.
22. Hopko, *The Orthodox Church: Worship*, 3.
23. Ibid., 3.

In some larger churches and cathedrals, this tradition of depicting "God is with us" is expressed by having a large icon of Christ *Pantocrator* (Christ, ruler of all) inside the central dome, or ceiling, of the church. Christ *Pantocrator* is holding the Gospel book in his left hand and blesses with his right hand. The icon portrays Christ as the Righteous Judge and the Lover of Mankind, both at the same time.

## The Interior of Orthodox Church Buildings

There are three primary parts to an Orthodox church. First, the narthex, the place where people walk in from the outside: the narthex represents the world. Here we are reminded of what God told Moses when Moses was to stand in his presence: "Do not draw near this place. Take your sandals off your feet, for the place where you stand is holy ground" (Exod 3:5 (NKJV)).[24] Second is the nave, or the body of the church, the space where the people of God gather for the liturgy. The nave is the largest section of the church, located between the narthex and the sanctuary. Finally, the sanctuary, or holy place, is where the priest prepares for and leads the liturgy. The sanctuary represents the Kingdom of God: "Lord, I have loved the habitation of Your house, and the place where Your glory dwells" (Ps 26:8 (NKJV)).

### ICONOSTASIS

An iconostasis, or icon screen, is a screen wall that separates the sanctuary from the nave. The iconostasis serves to show our unity with Christ, his Mother, and all the angels and

24. This section is informed by Hopko, *The Orthodox Church: Worship*, 4.

saints. The icons on the iconostasis also serve as witnesses to the presence of Christ's good news, the gospel of salvation.[25]

## ALTAR TABLE

Traditionally, in an Orthodox church the altar faces east, for the east represents light, truth, and what is good. The sun rises from the east and sets in the west. The altar not only symbolizes the Last Supper, but also the mystical presence of the heavenly throne, and so is also called the "Holy Throne" or "Holy Table," because the Lord is present on it.[26] It is also called the "Table of the Kingdom of God" (Luke 28:30)[27] and is described in Revelation this way:

> At once I was in the Spirit, and there before me was a throne in heaven with someone sitting on it . . . Surrounding the throne were twenty-four other thrones, and seated on them were twenty-four elders . . . In the center, around the throne, were four living creatures, and they were covered with eyes, in front and in back . . . Day and night they never stop saying: "Holy, holy, holy is the Lord God Almighty, who was, and is, and is to come." Whenever the living creatures give glory, honor and thanks to him who sits on the throne and who lives for ever and ever, the twenty-four elders fall down before him who sits on the throne, and worship him who lives for ever and ever. They lay their crowns before the throne and say: "You are worthy, our Lord and God, to re-

25. Ibid., 4.

26. Sokolof, *A Manual of the Orthodox Church's Divine Services*, 10.

27. Hopko, *The Orthodox Church: Worship*, 4.

ceive glory and honor and power, for you created all things, and by your will they were created and have their being" (Rev 4:2, 4, 6b, 8b–11 (NIV)).

## Icons

In A.D. 726, Byzantine Emperor Leo III initiated the Iconoclast controversy. The Iconoclasts ("icon-smashers") were suspicious of any religious art representing humans or God and demanded that such art be destroyed. The Iconodules ("icon-venerators"), on the other hand, were equally vigorous in their defense of icons in the life of the Church. Iconoclasts may have been influenced by Jewish and Muslim ideas ordering the removal of all images, but as Ware argues, ". . . within Christianity itself there had always existed a 'puritan' outlook, which condemned icons because it saw in all images a latent idolatry."[28] In A.D. 787, at the last Ecumenical Council before the final split between the church in the East and the church in the West, a declaration was issued that icons should be honored with the same veneration as the cross and the Holy Bible. Hopko explains the thinking behind this proclamation: "Icons bear witness to the reality of God's presence with us in the mystery of faith. The icons are not just human pictures or visual aids to contemplation and prayer. They are the witnesses of the presence of the Kingdom of God to us, and so of our own presence to the Kingdom of God in the Church."[29]

The nave of an Orthodox church holds many icons. These two-dimensional images of Jesus, Mary, or the saints,

28. Ware, *The Orthodox Church*, 31.
29. Hopko, *The Orthodox Church: Worship*, 12.

icons are not "religious" paintings; as stated above, they are understood to be witnesses to the truth. They are often described as "theology in colors and lines" or "windows to heaven." Orthodox Christians do not worship icons, nor do they worship the saints often depicted on them: only God is worshipped. Icons are, however, venerated or honored. They serve as a channel of grace of the spiritual presence of God and His saints, and the saints are not dead, but alive in Christ!

One of the best-known iconic images is that of Mary, standing with open arms, with the Christ child in front of her, framed in a large circle superimposed over her heart. This great evangelistic icon proclaims Christ living in Mary; and her outstretched arms invite us to let Him into our hearts as well.

Icons remind us that the saints also gather with us around the throne of God in heaven. In the Divine Liturgy, we ascend to heaven and join the saints in worshipping God: "I looked and heard the voice of many angels, numbering thousands upon thousands, and ten thousand times ten thousand. They encircled the throne and the living creatures and the elders. In a loud voice they sang: 'Worthy is the Lamb, who was slain, to receive power and wealth and wisdom and strength and honor and glory and praise!' Then I heard every creature in heaven and on earth and under the earth and on the sea, and all that is in them, singing: 'To him who sits on the throne and to the Lamb be praise and honor and glory and power, forever and ever.'" (Rev 5:11–13 (NIV)).

## THE LITURGY OF ST. JOHN CHRYSOSTOM

The most commonly celebrated liturgical form in the Orthodox Church is the Liturgy of St. John Chrysostom. This liturgy has existed in its present form—with some few variations—since the ninth century. It is comprised of two principal parts: (1) The Liturgy of the Catechumens, sometimes called the gathering or the *synaxis* (meaning a meeting in the church for liturgical purposes), at which the scriptures are proclaimed and expounded, and (2) The Liturgy of the Faithful, or the eucharistic sacrifice, in which the gifts of bread and wine are offered and consecrated.[30]

### The Liturgy of the Catechumens

The liturgy begins with a blessing: "Blessed is the Kingdom of the Father and of the Son and of the Holy Spirit." Thus, the liturgy begins with its end made explicit: the liturgy celebrated is ultimately a reflection of and participation in the glory of Heaven. The blessing is followed by the Litany of Peace, a series of prayers whose refrain is "Lord, have mercy." The antiphons (selections from the Psalms) are interspersed with shorter litanies. Then, while the choir sings the Beatitudes, the clergy make the "Little Entrance" carrying the gospel book from the altar, through the church, and back to the altar again. After the Little Entrance, the

---

30. Catechumens are those preparing for baptism or reception into the Orthodox Church. Other liturgical forms used by the Orthodox Church include the Liturgy of St. Basil the Great (the most ancient form of the liturgy, celebrated ten times every year), the Liturgy of St. James of Jerusalem (celebrated on his feast day), and the Liturgy of the Pre-sanctified Gifts (celebrated during Great Lent).

*Troparia* and *Kontakia* (a series of short hymns for the Sunday and any special church feast days) are sung, as is the "Thrice-Holy Hymn," an ancient hymn that mirrors the hymns of the angels around the heavenly throne of God. Passages from the apostolic writings (and sometimes from the Old Testament), interspersed with psalm verses, are read while the priest censes the church. Then the priest comes out from the altar and reads the gospel. A sermon usually follows. The Liturgy of the Catechumens concludes with more litanies.

## The Liturgy of the Faithful

After the short Litany of the Faithful and the censing of the church, the choir sings the "Cherubic Hymn," while the clergy solemnly make the "Great Entrance," carrying the bread and wine that will become the body and blood of Christ, from the "Table of Preparation," through the church, in the "Royal Doors," and to the "Holy Table." After another litany, the Creed is sung, reaffirming the tenets of the Orthodox faith. The priest then begins the *Anaphora* (Greek for "lifting up"), in which the congregation gives thanks to God for all that he has done. More specifically, the priest then recalls Christ's institution of the Eucharist and asks that the Father send the Holy Spirit to make the bread and wine into the precious body and blood of Christ. Following another litany, the Lord's Prayer is sung. The clergy and people then say pre-Communion prayers together. The choir sings a selection of hymns, while first the clergy and then the faithful receive the Eucharist "for the healing of soul and body." This is the center of the worship, the sacrament that unites each person with every other, with all the saints who have ever lived, and with Christ himself. When all have received, the priest returns the body and blood to the Table of Preparation while the choir sings hymns of thanksgiving. The liturgy proper concludes with final prayers and blessings.

| Catholic Liturgy | The Liturgy of St. John Chrysostom |
|---|---|
| **Liturgy of the Word** | **Liturgy of the Catechumens** |
| Greeting | Blessed be the Kingdom |
| Rite of Blessing | Great Litany |
| Penitential Rite | First Antiphon |
| Kyrie | Short Litany |
| Gloria | Second Antiphon |
| Opening Prayer | Short Litany |
| Old Testament | Third Antiphon |
| Psalm | Small Entrance |
| New Testament Epistle | *Troparion and Kontakion* |
| Alleluia | *Trisagion* |
| Gospel | Old Testament |
| Homily | New Testament Epistle (Optional) |
| Creed | Gospel |
| Intercessions | Homily |
| | The Litany of Fervent Supplication |
| | The Litany of the Departed |
| | The Litany of the Catechumens |

| Liturgy of the Eucharist | Liturgy of the Faithful |
|---|---|
| | First Prayer of the Faithful |
| Presentation of Bread and Wine | Second Prayer of the Faithful |
| | Cherubic Hymn |
| Prayer over the Gifts | Great Entrance |
| Eucharistic Prayer | Litany of Supplication |
| The Lord's Prayer | Prayer of the Offering |
| Peace | Peace |
| Breaking of the Bread | Creed |
| Communion | Anaphora |
| Prayer after Communion | Hymn to the Theotokos |
| Concluding Rite Greeting | Litany before the Lord's Prayer |
| | Lord's Prayer |
| Blessing | Communion |
| Dismissal | Litany of Thanksgiving |
| | The Prayer before the Ambo |
| | The Dismissal |

## THE LITURGICAL YEAR

Like the Catholic Church and other Western church denominations, the Orthodox Church follows a liturgical year; its year differs from them, however, in two significant ways. The liturgical year of the Orthodox Church begins on September 1 instead of the first Sunday of Advent. Second, its lectionary is a one-year cycle of readings, repeated year after year, in contrast to the Western three-year cycles of readings.

## Pascha

The most important feast day in the Orthodox calendar is *Pascha* (Easter), the day that celebrates the resurrection of Christ. In Hebrew, *pascha* means "passing over" or deliverance." In the Old Testament, the Passover commemorates the great exodus of the Jews from Egypt: The LORD said to Moses and Aaron in Egypt, "This month is to be for you the first month, the first month of your year. Tell the whole community of Israel that on the tenth day of this month each man is to take a lamb for his family, one for each household. The animals you choose must be year-old males without defect, and you may take them from the sheep or the goats. Take care of them until the fourteenth day of the month, when all the people of the community of Israel must slaughter them at twilight. Then they are to take some of the blood and put it on the sides and tops of the doorframes of the houses where they eat the lambs. Eat it in haste; it is the LORD's Passover. On that same night I will pass through Egypt and strike down every firstborn—both men and animals—and I will bring judgment on all the gods of Egypt. I am the LORD. The blood will be a sign for you on the houses where you are; and when I see the blood, I will pass over you. No destructive plague will touch you when I strike Egypt" (Exod 12: 1–2, 5–7, 11–13 (NIV)).

In his book, *Orthodox Christianity*, Carl S. Tyneh explains that "Christians, celebrating the New Testament Pascha, exult in the deliverance through Christ of all the people from slavery to the devil and in granting of Life and everlasting bliss. As sung in the canons: 'From death to Life and from the earth to the Heavens hath Christ God brought us.'"[31] Hopko reinforces this idea when he writes: "[T]he real liturgical center of the annual cycle of Orthodox worship is the feast of the Resurrection of Christ. All elements of Orthodox liturgical piety point to and flow from Easter, the celebration of the New Christian Passover."[32] This theological concept is enthusiastically articulated in song during the *Pascha* liturgy as the traditional Easter *Troparion* is sung: "Christ is risen from the dead, trampling down death by death, and upon those in the tombs bestowing life."

## The Twelve Great Feast Days

While *Pascha* is the central moment of the Orthodox calendar, the year is punctuated by twelve major feast days. As Hopko explains (above), these feast days, which commemorate the lives of Christ and the *Theotokos* (Mary, the Mother of God) lead up to and flow out of Christ's resurrection, celebrated in *Pascha*. Nine of the major feast days are "fixed"; i.e., they fall on specific dates. Three of the major feast days—in addition to *Pascha*—have moveable dates, dates which change from year to year depending on the dates of the spring equinox and the Jewish Passover.[33]

31. Tyneh, *Orthodox Christianity*, 129.

32. Hopko, *The Orthodox Church: Worship*, 70.

33. For more information on the date of Pascha, see Lewis J. Patsavos, "Dating Pascha in the Orthodox Church."

34. "Church Year."

**MAJOR FEASTS OF THE ORTHODOX CHURCH**[34]
**FEASTS THAT FALL ON FIXED DATES:**

| | |
|---|---|
| September 8 | The Nativity of Mary the *Theotokos* |
| September 14 | The Exaltation of the Cross |
| November 21 | The Presentation of the *Theotokos* to the Temple |
| December 25 | The Nativity of Christ |
| January 6 | The Epiphany: The Baptism of Christ |
| February 2 | The Meeting of Christ in the Temple |
| March 25 | The Annunciation |
| August 6 | The Transfiguration of Christ |
| August 15 | The Dormition of the *Theotokos* |

**FEASTS WHOSE DATES ARE SET ACCORDING TO THE SPRING EQUINOX AND THE JEWISH PASSOVER:**[35]

| | |
|---|---|
| Palm Sunday | The Entry into Jerusalem |
| PASCHA | CHRIST'S RESURRECTION |
| Ascension | The Ascension of Christ |
| Pentecost | The Descent of the Holy Spirit |

35. For more information re the difference between the Old (Julian) Calendar and the New (Gregorian) Calendar, which is used by the Western church, see Lewis J. Patsavos, "The Calendar of the Orthodox Church."

# 4

## The Historically Orthodox
## Evangelical Perspective

### THE SACRAMENT OF PREACHING

As we have seen, Catholics and Orthodox Christians believe that there are seven sacraments: Evangelicals and all other Protestants accept only two. While the theological debate about, and differences in, the understanding and number of these sacraments is surely important, the larger issue being raised in this chapter is the broader sacramental character of the Christian life; hence, this examination of the "sacrament" of preaching for orthodox Evangelicals.

In *Systematic Theology: Life in the Spirit*, Thomas C. Oden asserts that the most important sacrament of the Church is preaching. He writes: "The most crucial sign of the church in the Protestant tradition is the pure preaching of God's Word, a right profession of the true, pure and rightly understood doctrine of the law and the gospel. God's people cannot be without God's Word, nor can God's Word be without a people. The surest mark of the true church is that in it one hears the pure gospel proclaimed."[1]

---

1. Oden, *Life in the Spirit*, 299.

## The Evangelical Nature of Pauline Preaching

In *Essentials of Evangelical Thought*, Donald G. Bloesch develops this same concept and argues that the preaching of Paul was both sacramental and evangelical. In Rom 10:14–17, Paul states that people come to salvation through the preaching of the Gospel.[2] "But how are they to call on one in whom they have not believed? And how are they to believe in one of whom they have never heard? And how are they to hear without someone to proclaim him? And how are they to proclaim him unless they are sent? As it is written, 'How beautiful are the feet of those who bring good news!' But not all have obeyed the good news; for Isaiah says, 'Lord, who has believed our message?' So faith comes from what is heard, and what is heard comes through the word of Christ" (NRSV). He says again in 1 Corinthians (1:21): "For since, in the wisdom of God, the world did not know God through wisdom, God decided, through the foolishness of our proclamation, to save those who believe" (NRSV).

Moreover, in 1 Cor. 9:16, Paul also writes that he saw himself ". . . under a divine mandate to preach and he knew that he would fall under divine judgment if he spurned this injunction."[3] He states: "If I proclaim the gospel, this gives me no ground for boasting, for an obligation is laid on me, and woe betide me if I do not proclaim the gospel" (NRSV).[4]

---

2. Bloesch, *Essentials of Evangelical Theology*, Vol. 2, 72.

3. Bloesch, *Essentials of Evangelical Theology*, Vol. 2, 73.

4. From a pedagogical perspective, the preaching of God's Word is the primary and, often, the only form of religious education that many people receive. Preaching serves as a powerful form of sharing

## WORD AND SACRAMENT

For Catholics and Orthodox Christians, the Eucharist is the source and center of Christian life; therefore, in their liturgies, the Word is subordinate to the Eucharist. For traditional Evangelicals, on the other hand, the Word is the source and center of Christian life; therefore, in their worship, the Lord's Supper is subordinate to the Word. So how do orthodox Evangelicals view the relationship between Word and Sacrament?

Orthodox Evangelicals are passionately committed to recovering what Bloesch calls the "catholic substance" of the liturgy and the Lord's Supper. He writes: "It is not only the preached Word but also the celebration of the sacraments that creates and sustains the fellowship of Christ . . . In addition to upholding evangelical distinctives, we need to regain catholic substance, which means continuity with the tradition of the whole church, including its sacramental side . . . We need to see [sacraments] as visible testimonies or signs of what God has done for us in Christ, signs in which the Holy Spirit is active in applying the benefits of Christ's death and resurrection . . . conservative evangelical Christianity has lost sight of the divine side in the sacraments . . ."[5]

Oden considers the practice of the sacraments not only a visible sign of the Church, but a condition of the Church's existence. He argues: "Because intentionally instituted by the Lord, there can be no church without a fitting

---

and passing on the faith. Therefore, the recovery of evangelical, Christocentric preaching is imperative. This idea will be developed further in the final chapter.

5. Bloesch, *Essentials of Evangelical Theology*, Vol. 2, 89, 278–279.

sacramental life . . . Where there is no one baptized, there is no church. Where the farewell meal is uncelebrated, one has no right to expect the true church."[6]

Furthermore, without a developed and ongoing celebration of the sacraments, too much importance is placed on the personality and gifts of the preacher instead of the mystery of the liturgy. Robert Webber suggests that ". . . part of the problem is that we have made our [Evangelical] churches into centers of evangelism and instruction. The focus of our services is on man and his needs instead of God and his glory."[7] P. T. Forsyth claims that preaching is a part of worship—indeed, that it is worship. But worship is *not* reducible to preaching. Forsyth states: "It [preaching] has lost power because it has been made the chief or only function of the Church, which is really to worship."[8]

Historically orthodox Evangelicals understand the sacraments to be ". . . the visible form of the Word . . . ,"[9] but believe that although they are integral components of Christian faith and growth, the sacraments can never substitute for the Word. In contrast to the understanding of Catholic and Orthodox theology, i.e., that the sacraments are grace-infused, both orthodox and traditional Evangelicals believe that salvation comes not from the sacraments, but from responding to God's Word. Bloesch explains: "While the sacraments are supremely helpful in the application of the fruits of salvation, the Word alone is indispensable for salvation. There is no fullness of the Church without the

6. Oden, *Life in the Spirit*, 300.

7. Webber, "Agenda for the Church," 15.

8. P. T. Forsyth, *Congregationalism and Reunion*, 78.

9. Bloesch, *Essentials of Evangelical Theology*, Vol. 2, 89.

sacraments, but there can be true fellowships of believers apart from the sacraments."[10]

Oden is even more direct in connecting preaching with regeneration, or the new birth. He writes: "New birth comes from hearing the Gospel . . . The Spirit works immediately in the heart and mediately through the word addressed in scripture and sacraments . . . Paul reminded the Corinthians that they had been personally born into the Christian community through his preaching . . . Enabling the hearing of the word written and word preached, the Spirit draws persons toward union with Christ through the preached word, repentance, faith, conversion and perseverance."[11] This notion is also reflected in the teachings of Luther and Calvin, who both held a high view of the sacraments. Bloesch quotes Luther: "For the word can exist without the sacraments, but the sacraments cannot exist without the word. And in the case of necessity, a man can be saved without the sacrament, but not without the word; this is true of those who desire baptism but die before that can receive it."[12]

Bloesch also cites Calvin, who proclaimed: "I do not, indeed, deny that the grace of Christ is applied to us in the sacraments, and that our reconciliation with God is then confirmed in our consciences; but, as the testimony of the Gospel is engraven upon the sacraments, they are not to be judged separately by themselves, but must be taken in connection with the Gospel, of which they are appendages."[13]

10. Bloesch, *Essentials of Evangelical Theology*, Vol. 2, 89.

11. Oden, *Life in the Spirit*, 165.

12. Bloesch, *Essentials of Evangelical Theology*, Vol. 2, 89–90; see also Luther, *D. Martin Luther's Werke*, 10, 1, 1, 387.

13. Ibid., 90; see also Calvin, *Commentary on the Epistles of Paul*

It could be argued by some that the sacraments, particularly the connection made between the liturgical sacraments of Eucharist and Holy Orders, have become divisive,
an obstacle to Church unity. It is the Holy Bible, the sacred
Scripture, the Word of God that brings Christians together.
Nevertheless, while Oden agrees that the question of Holy
Orders may divide and the Scriptures unite, he is quick to
affirm the integral place of the sacraments within the life of
the liturgical worshipping community: "Word is logically
and theologically prior to sacrament . . . for the essential
efficacy of the sacraments is the Word that enlivens. Yet we
are rightly reminded by liturgical traditions that it is always
the community to which the sacraments are entrusted that
proclaims the preached word and that the bath and meal
were firmly established before Pentecost."[14]

## THE PARADOXICAL TENSION FOR
## ORTHODOX EVANGELICALS BETWEEN THE
## SACRAMENTS AND SACERDOTALISM

While recognizing that ordination is an apostolate of leadership, traditional and orthodox Evangelicals do not accept ordination as a sacrament. This is a clear break with
Catholic and Orthodox theology. For Evangelicals, belief in
the priesthood of believers gives authority to all people to
preach the gospel. Bloesch agrees with the teaching of Hans
Küng, the great twentieth-century Catholic theologian, on
the topic of ordination. Bloesch writes: "For Küng, the fundamental apostolic succession is that of the Church itself
and of every Christian and consists of an objective keeping

*the Apostle to the Corinthians*, 239.

14. Oden, *Life in the Spirit*, 301.

of the faith of the apostles, which must be concretely realized ever again . . . Reformed Christianity would heartily
concur in this view that those preachers who remain faithful to the apostolic message stand in apostolic succession.[15]

Rooted in this understanding, orthodox Evangelicals
stand in the tension of a paradox. They desire and promote
a recovery of sacramental integrity, on the one hand; yet,
because of their theological interpretations regarding the
clerical priesthood, Evangelicals are cautious, if not suspicious of it. For Evangelicals, since Jesus Christ is the High
Priest whom we approach directly, there is no longer a need
for priests. There is no more need for a human mediator.

As mentioned in Chapter 1, neither traditional nor
orthodox Evangelicals believe the sacraments are salvific,
whereas Catholic theology understands the sacrament of
Baptism to be regenerative: it is the new birth. Furthermore,
the sacraments are understood as necessary for salvation[16].
Moreover, Catholic theology teaches that the priest serves
as a mediator between God and humanity; that it is through
the priest, as the channel, that the grace of God is infused in
human beings in Baptism and the Eucharist, for the priest
is the representation of Christ.

While embracing both of these sacraments, most
orthodox Evangelicals would not accept this teaching, i.e.,
sacerdotalism. Orthodox Evangelicals, for example, believe
that baptism, joined with repentance and faith, becomes the
means by which people receive the gift of regeneration.[17] As
Bloesch emphasizes: "Baptism by itself is not indispensable

15. Bloesch, *Essentials of Evangelical Theology*, Vol. 2, 120.

16. *CCC*, para. 1129.

17. Bloesch, *Essentials of Evangelical Theology*, 12.

for salvation . . . The Word of God alone is the indispensable means of salvation, while baptism is the aid."[18] Baptism is rather the sign and seal of the new birth in Christ. Baptism is the outward sign, and the Spirit is the inward sign. In this, Oden concurs with Bloesch. While affirming the inseparable nature of Baptism with regeneration, Oden also views them as distinguishable:

> It is not baptism of itself that saves; but God through grace who enables repentance and faith, of which baptism is a primary *musterion, sacramentum*, sacramental act, sign and evidence . . . An oversimplified identification of baptism and a new birth, often called baptismal regeneration, seems to be placed in question by scriptural instances of people being regenerated who seemingly were not baptized (the thief in Lk 23:42, 43; Cornelius in Acts 10:44, 48), and of persons who were baptized but apparently unregenerated (Simon Magus in Acts 8:13–23; Ananias and Sapphira in Acts 5:1–11). Hence, though not separable, baptism and regeneration are in some instances distinguishable.[19]

And herein lies another paradoxical tension. Although orthodox Evangelicals reject the idea that Baptism is in its nature salvific and regenerative, they do baptize infants. This is a break with traditional Evangelical theology, which emphasizes Believer's Baptism. Bloesch explains the position of historically orthodox Evangelicals this way:

---

18. Ibid., 91.

19. Oden, *Life in the Spirit*, 170–171.

> The Holy Spirit is indeed working upon a person at baptism, even upon an infant, but he does not make his abode within the person until the decision of faith. Our new birth can be said to be initiated at baptism (in the case of infants), but it is not fulfilled until conversion. In the case of adults who are already believers, baptism is a confirmation of their conversion. We can say that baptism is not a condition of salvation but a preparation for it in some cases and a certification of it in others . . . Conversion is indeed a ripening process but only after the new birth has taken place. Infants cannot be said to be regenerated, for they lack conscious faith in Jesus Christ. At the same time, if they have been baptized, we can say that they are under the claim of divine election and are within the sphere of the kingdom of God.[20]

Oden expands this discussion by emphasizing the work of the Spirit in the lives of infants and children. He argues that while children may not have conscious justifying faith, they do have proleptic (anticipating) faith. He elaborates:

> One is equally correct in saying that faith leads to baptism and baptism leads to faith, for faith and baptism are interdependent teachings . . . Baptism is more than a public act of confession or a public testimony to one's faith. Conversely, baptism of itself is no substitute for active faith or faith becoming active in love. As penitent, trusting acceptance of grace, faith is an assumed

20. Bloesch, *Essentials of Evangelical Theology*, Vol. 2, 14, 91.

condition of baptism. This is arguable even in the case of infant baptism on the premise that grace is being received proleptically through the faith of caring parents within the covenant community . . . Most agree that God the Spirit works within the lives of infants in a different way than adults. Whether consciously in adults through justifying grace or preliminarily in infants through prevenient grace, faith itself can never become a meritorious cause or ground, but only the ordered way of receiving grace. However the debates on infant baptism may proceed, the question of God's power to work on infants hinges not on neonate capacity or activity but the divine determination to call and shape human life rightly from the beginning, hence prevenient grace . . . When Jesus called a little child and had him stand among them, he delivered one of his most memorable teachings: ". . . if anyone cause one of these little ones who believe in me to sin it would be better to have a large millstone hung around his neck and to be drowned in the depths of the sea (Mt. 18:2–6). Even the little child here appears to be capable of proleptic belief in God's coming. Such "little children" carried in the arms of their parents were called to come to God the Son: "Let the little children come to me, and do not hinder them, for the kingdom of God belongs to such as these" (Mk. 10:13, 14)."[21]

Orthodox Evangelicals would reject the sacramental presumption the *Catechism of the Catholic Church* makes that infants who have died without being baptized may not

21. Oden, *Life in the Spirit*, 173–174.

receive salvation. The *CCC* states that "As regards children who have died without baptism, the Church can only entrust them to the mercy of God, as she does in her funeral rites for them. Indeed, the great mercy of God who desires that all men should be saved . . . All the more urgent is the Church's call not to prevent little children coming to Christ through the gift of holy Baptism."[22]

Historically orthodox Evangelicals recognize that the church is an institution with a structure and sacred tradition. Therefore, in order to develop what Bloesch calls a "catholic balance," they consider that the position of ministerial leadership should be viewed as deriving its authority from God and also through the priesthood of believers. "The ministry of the Word and sacraments must not be downgraded (as in a spiritualistic egalitarianism), but it must not be unduly elevated (as in sacerdotalism)."[23] The church is a sacramental and ecclesiastical institution.

On the one hand, the theological concept of the priesthood of believers must be vigorously re-infused into the life of the church. According to Bloesch, "[w]e need to recover the biblical and catholic doctrine of the royal priesthood of the church . . . All Christians are called to the apostolate and not just those who are commissioned to oversee congregations. All Christians are summoned to sacrifice themselves for the salvation of the world and the advancement of the kingdom of God in the world. Every Christian should be an evangelist, in the sense that he is placed under the divine obligation to give testimony to his faith before the world."[24]

22. *CCC*, para. 1261.

23. Bloesch, *Essentials of Evangelical Theology*, Vol. 2, 125.

24. Ibid., 126.

On the other hand, ordained ministerial leadership is essential for the life and health of the Body of Christ. This is particularly significant for orthodox Evangelicals, who seek to recover the sacraments and sacred tradition. Bloesch continues: "Two of the hallmarks of the church are the preaching of the Word and the right administration of the sacraments . . . Baptism is conceived not only as an entrance into the body of the church but as dedication to the conversion of the world . . . The Lord's Supper is not just a memorial of Christ's past sacrifice but a participation in his present intercession for the sins of the world . . . Sacramental celebration should not be reduced to fellowship or agape meal, for it signifies a real participation in the body and blood of Christ."[25]

## RECOVERING THE HISTORICAL FULLNESS OF CHRISTIAN WORSHIP

### The Enlightenment

Since the Enlightenment, a number of philosophical beliefs have dominated the Western understanding of human beings, of God, and of worship. Four of the most significant philosophical perspectives have been those of Isaac Newton, Charles Darwin, Sigmund Freud, and Karl Marx.

The teachings of Isaac Newton emphasize an anti-supernatural, rationalistic perspective on life. "The Newtonian view of life relegates God to the heavens and rejects an active presence of God in worship."[26] However,

25. Ibid., 91.
26. Webber, *Blended Worship*, 19.

informed by Thomas Kuhn's *The Structures of Scientific Revolutions*, Robert Webber claims that ". . . with the demise of a Newtonian outlook that sees the world as standing still, we are witnessing the end of a faith and worship characterized by passive noninvolvement, intellectualized propositions and a seeming absence of God."[27]

Charles Darwin argues that human beings evolved from a lower species, and thus challenges the pre-modern assumption that God created human beings. With the work of Darwin, Webber suggests, "a new doctrine of creation was born."[28] Sigmund Freud opines that religion is the invention of the human imagination, and that therefore humans can reject religious notions and stand on their own two feet, to face life with courage and to create meaning. In the writings of Sigmund Freud, Webber says, "a new doctrine of salvation was made."[29] Finally, Karl Marx believes that human beings must take history into their own hands, eliminate the competition between rich and poor, and recreate a communal society. In this, Webber sees that ". . . a new doctrine of the future was born."[30] From these and other notions issuing from the Enlightenment, the modern concepts of science, reason, and evidence emerged.

27. Ibid., 19; see also, Kuhn, *The Structure of Scientific Revolutions*.

28. Webber, *Blended Worship*, 20.

29. Ibid., 20.

30. Ibid., 20.

## The Response of Evangelical Worship
## to the Enlightenment

In terms of worship, the initial reaction of traditional Evangelicals to the Enlightenment was to develop an ". . . intellectual worship service."[31] Because many of them adopted the Enlightenment notion that God does not intervene supernaturally in the world today in the same way as in biblical times, Evangelicals did not seek anything supernatural in this type of worship service. They believed that the primary task of the church is to defend the Christian faith, and that "[t]hrough the use of science, reason and empirical evidence, the church can prove this to be a supernatural world."[32] The pastor who shared this perspective used the pulpit to proclaim the evidence of faith. Worship became schooling, and sermons became intellectual lessons arguing propositions on faith.

The second historical reaction to the Enlightenment regarding worship was the development of an "emotional worship service."[33] For those who share this perspective, the Christian faith is something to be experienced, not argued or debated; indeed, many believe the mind to be the enemy of the Church. These so-called "enthusiasts" want a Christianity "that touches the heart, moves the will, and results in holy living. They want commitment and passion. They want to feel the presence of Christ and the power of the Holy Spirit."[34] The experiences and traditions of the Pietists, the Revivalists, the Holiness Movement, the Black

31. Ibid., 22.
32. Ibid., 22
33. Ibid., 22.
34. Ibid., 24.

Church, the Pentecostals, and the Charismatics find their roots in this view of worship. This type of worship is highly emotive, includes passionate sermons, and aims to engender an emotional response. At the end of the worship service, there is usually a public call to repentance, popularly dubbed the "Altar Call."

These two opposing historical Evangelical responses to the Enlightenment have led to three contemporary worship styles: (1) the traditional Protestant worship style; (2) the praise-and-worship/charismatic worship style; and (3) the creative/contemporary worship style.

The traditional Protestant worship style emphasizes classic Protestant hymns from the Reformation, prayers said aloud, and the preaching of the Word. Distinctive denominational elements and traditions are apparent in this worship style. The order of services tends not to be as fixed as in the liturgical traditions of the Catholic or Orthodox Churches nor as free as the more extemporaneous style of worship.

The praise-and-worship/charismatic worship style reflects the spirit of the historical emotional Revivalist worship response. This worship style emphasizes openness to the Spirit, which has led to much freedom of expression, including people lifting their hands, dancing in the Spirit and, if so moved, speaking in tongues. The use of personal testimonials of lives changed through Jesus Christ is also a standard, and powerful, aspect of this worship style.

Finally, the creative/contemporary style provides an abbreviated and contemporized version of the traditional worship style, with an intentional emphasis on the experiential, seen as more relevant and attractive to postmodern sensibilities. This worship style encourages the use of drama, movies, and references to popular books and cultural norms that reflect the day-to-day realities of most participants. Contemporary Christian music commonly accompanies this style of worship.

## A NEW, DYNAMIC VIEW OF WORSHIP

There is a new view of worship. According to Webber, "[t]he single most important thing the church can do is worship. A vibrant worship life will break through the sense that God is absent and reach the people in the world who are searching for meaning."[35] Webber explains that in *A Brief History of Time*, Stephen Hawking describes ". . . the shift between the old Newtonian mechanistic and rationalistic world [and] a new world view that recognizes the complexity and dynamic nature of all things."[36] Hawking claims, and Webber agrees, that the universe is no longer understood as static and unchanging. Rather, it is dynamic and expanding. According to Webber's reading of Hawking, the universe must have had a beginning, will have an ending, and likely has a creator.[37] Webber punctuates the importance of this insight in relation to worship: ". . . people are now considerably more open to the supernatural and are searching for an experience of mystery. They are convinced of the interrelatedness of all things and are more community-oriented and more process-oriented and are given to learning and communicating through the visual."[38]

---

35. Webber, *Blended Worship*, 19.

36. Ibid., 26; see also Hawking, *A Brief History of Time*.

37. Webber, *Blended Worship*, 26.

38. Ibid., 26.

This dynamic and open universal perspective poses challenges to the Christian church, in particular given the rise of the popular New Age Movement. However these challenges may also be opportunities. According to Webber, "[t]he challenge is to express and practice a biblical Christianity and worship . . . We cannot meet the challenge with a Christianity shaped by the Enlightenment. Neither a liberal mythological faith, a conservative intellectualized faith or an emotional faith lacking in content will adequately address New Age issues. A faith grounded in the Bible proclaims an open universe in which the supernatural does occur and things are interrelated through God's act of Creation."[39]

## Defining Christian Worship

Recognizing the new forms of worship emerging from new, post-Enlightenment perspectives, Webber provides the following insightful definitional understanding of Christian worship:

> Worship represents Jesus Christ through re-presentation. Worship tells and acts out the living, dying and rising of Christ. Worship celebrates Christ's victory over evil, the certain doom of Satan, and the promise of a new heaven and a new earth. A brief yet comprehensive definition of worship is [that] worship celebrates God's saving deed in Jesus Christ. This worship is not goal-driven worship, but a Christ-driven worship. And when Christ is the center of worship, all of the goals for worship are achieved: Christ

39. Ibid., 24.

centered worship educates, evangelizes, heals, develops spirituality and is most enjoyable. A Christ-centered worship—which is event-driven worship—can never be static and merely intellectual because what happens is an actual and real communication of the power and benefit of the life, death and resurrection of Christ.[40]

## Recovering the Language of Liturgical Worship

Conceptual language such as the relationship of words, logic, reading, writing, abstraction, strictness, intelligence, clarity, analysis and linear sequence[41]—dominated the Enlightenment and the modern age and likewise their language and forms of worship. In the post-Enlightenment or post-modern age in which we live, it may be that symbolic language—including images, knowledge by participation and immersion, primacy of experience, environment, global perception, sensitivity to signs and indicators and sensitivity to the spiritual—better reflects the new dynamic view of worship.

The Evangelical understanding of worship is still rooted in modernity's conceptual language. Webber would argue that the way to recover the fullness of Christian worship relevant to post-moderns, while yet remaining "Evangelical," is to develop a language of communication that integrates both conceptual and symbolic forms. The liturgical worship style, discussed below, seems to Webber to be the best model for integrating both conceptual language (Word) and symbolic language (Eucharist).

40. Ibid., 24.
41. Ibid., 105.

## Liturgical Worship: Integrating Conceptual and Symbolic Language[42]

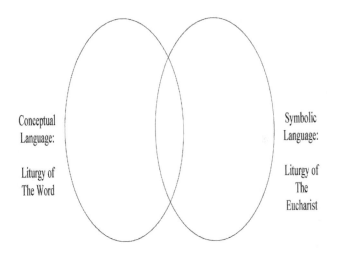

Conceptual
Language:

Liturgy of
The Word

Symbolic
Language:

Liturgy of
The
Eucharist

The movement from the conceptual to the symbolic actually highlights a return to the ancient language and forms of worship communication of the early church. This return to classical Christian understanding is at the heart of Webber's "Ancient-Future" modality.[43]

The figure below presents a comparison of the central ideas of each paradigm of church history and the correspondence between ideas of the ancient church and the post-modern church.[44]

42. Ibid., 34. See also Babin, *The New Era in Religious Communication*, 150–151.

43. Webber uses the term "ancient-future" as a way to connect early church teachings and models with the post-modern church. See Webber, *Ancient-Future Faith*; *Ancient-Future Evangelism*; *Ancient-Future Time*.

44. Webber, *Ancient-Future Faith*, 34.

| PARADIGMS OF CHURCH HISTORY[1] | | | | |
|---|---|---|---|---|
| **Ancient** | **Medieval** | **Refor-mation** | **Modern** | **Post-modern** |
| Mystery Comm -unity Symbol | Institu-tional | Word | Reason Systematic and Analytical Verbal Individualistic | Mystery Community Symbol |

## LITURGICAL WORSHIP IN THE EARLY CHURCH

From the time of the early church, Christians have celebrated worship focused around the Word and the Eucharist.[45] In Acts 2:42, we see the classic biblical model of Christian worship. It includes fellowship, listening to the apostles' teaching, breaking bread, prayers, and sharing possessions and funds: "They devoted themselves to the apostles' teaching and fellowship, to the breaking of bread and the prayers" (NRSV).

The *Didache* or the *Teaching of the Twelve Disciples*, a manual for Christian instruction written sometime early in the second century, shows that Christians celebrated the Eucharist "every Lord's Day" (Chapter XIV, v. 1), and that only those baptized are permitted to partake of the Eucharist (Chapter IX, v. 5). Following are excerpts from Chapters 9, 10, and 14 of the *Didache*, which specifically discuss the Eucharist and the Lord's Day.[46]

45. Webber, *Blended Worship*, 24.

46. "Didache," in *The Apostolic Fathers*, 303–334. See also "The Teaching of the Twelve Apostles."

*Chapter IX. The Thanksgiving (Eucharist)*

1. Now concerning the Thanksgiving (Eucharist), thus give thanks. 2. First, concerning the cup: We thank thee, our Father, for the holy vine of David Thy servant, which Thou madest known to us through Jesus Thy Servant; to Thee be the glory for ever. 3. And concerning the broken bread: We thank Thee, our Father, for the life and knowledge which Thou madest known to us through Jesus Thy Servant; to Thee be the glory for ever. 4. Even as this broken bread was scattered over the hills, and was gathered together and became one, so let Thy Church be gathered together from the ends of the earth into Thy kingdom; for Thine is the glory and the power through Jesus Christ for ever. 5. But let no one eat or drink of your Thanksgiving (Eucharist), but they who have been baptized into the name of the Lord; for concerning this also the Lord hath said, Give not that which is holy to the dogs.

*Chapter X. Prayer After Communion.*

1. But after ye are filled, thus give thanks: 2. We thank Thee, holy Father, for Thy holy name which Thou didst cause to tabernacle in our hearts, and for the knowledge and faith and immortality, which Thou madest known to us through Jesus Thy Servant; to Thee be the glory for ever. 3. Thou, Master almighty, didst create all things for Thy name's sake; Thou gavest food and drink to men for enjoyment, that they might give thanks to Thee; but to us Thou didst freely give spiritual food and drink and life eternal through Thy Servant. 4. Before all things we thank Thee that Thou art

mighty; to Thee be the glory for ever. 5. Remember, Lord, Thy Church, to deliver it from all evil and to make it perfect in Thy love, and gather it from the four winds, sanctified for Thy kingdom which Thou hast prepared for it; for Thine is the power and the glory for ever. 6. Let grace come, and let this world pass away. Hosanna to the God (Son) of David! If any one is holy, let him come; if any one is not so, let him repent. Maranatha. Amen. 7. But permit the prophets to make Thanksgiving as much as they desire.

*Chapter XIV. Christian Assembly on the Lord's Day.*

1. But every Lord's day do ye gather yourselves together, and break bread, and give thanksgiving after having confessed your transgressions, that your sacrifice may be pure. But let no one that is at variance with his fellow come together with you, until they be reconciled, that your sacrifice may not be profaned. 3. For this is that which was spoken by the Lord: In every place and time offer to me a pure sacrifice; for I am a great King, saith the Lord, and my name is wonderful among the nations.

It is essential to note the proximity of the composition of the Acts of the Apostles and the *Didache*. Bruce Metzger and Roland Murphy place the composition of Acts as early as A.D. 65–67 and as late as A.D. 80.[47] Richard Dillon suggests it was more likely between A.D. 80–90.[48] The *Didache* is considered a composite document: Part One, comprising chapters I to VI, is called "The Two Ways." Part Two, comprising chapters VII to XVI, is called "The Teaching."

47. "The Acts of the Apostles," 160.
48. Dillon et al, "Acts of the Apostles."

According to Kirsopp Lake, The Two Ways may have been written early in the first century and The Teaching early in the second century.[49] Cyril E. Richardson, on the other hand, firmly asserts that the *Didache* is a second-century document.[50] It would appear, therefore, that the *Didache*'s articulation of the teaching with respect to the Eucharist was written within one hundred years of the composition of the Acts of the Apostles. This seems to imply that the Eucharist, together with the Word, was a standard part of Christian worship during the early church.

## The Shape and Movements of Liturgical Worship

Liturgical worship is composed of two overarching parts: Word and Eucharist. In his book, *Liturgical Theology*, Simon Chan, an Asian Pentecostal theologian in the historically orthodox tradition, explains the significance of Word and Eucharist within the context of Christian worship:

> The church throughout its history has recognized that this basic ordo consists of two parts, Word and sacrament. This two-part shape could be explored from a number of perspectives. First . . . both have their basis in the Incarnation, the Word becoming flesh. Thus Christ could be called the "primordial Sacrament," and all true worship is fundamentally sacramental. Second, within the sacramental framework of worship, the Eucharist holds a special place as the "sacra-

49. Lake, "Didache: The Teaching of the Twelve Apostles," 307.

50. Richardson, "The Teaching of the Twelve Apostles"; See also "The Teaching of the Twelve Apostles," in Christian Classics Ethereal Library.

ment of sacraments." It is from the Eucharist that we come to a better understanding of the church as essentially communion. The liturgy, then, has a Eucharistic orientation. Third, the Eucharist, which communicates the eternal reality, is always celebrated in time, in daily, weekly and yearly circles. This means that within the liturgy, eternity and time, the "already and not yet," are set in an eschatological tension, giving to the liturgy an eschatological orientation. Fourth, the liturgy of the Word and sacrament is set within two other essential acts: the gathering for worship and the sending forth into the world. This pattern reveals its missiological orientation.[51]

In his examination of liturgical worship, Chan revisits the classic formula, *lex orandi est lex credendi*. He believes there is a dialectical relationship between the rule of praying and the rule of belief, but that worship and doctrine ". . . are so inextricably linked that separation can only undermine the integrity of both doctrine and worship. Yet this divorce is exactly what we are seeing in many evangelical churches."[52] In many Evangelical worship services, the celebration of the Lord's Supper is simply an obligatory, but perfunctory, addendum to the worship service. The result, as Chan's states, ". . . is a divorce between worship and theology, leaving both impoverished."[53]

The four movements of liturgical worship are presented in the following figure. Orthodox Evangelicals propose this four-movement liturgical service as the primary Sunday order of worship.

51. Chan, *Liturgical Theology*, 63.
52. Ibid., 52.
53. Ibid., 52.

| THE FOUR MOVEMENTS OF WORSHIP | | | |
|---|---|---|---|
| THE LITURGY OF THE WORD | | THE LITURGY OF THE EUCHARIST | |
| GATHERING | WORD | EUCHARIST | DISMISSAL |
| We enter into God's presence | We hear God's Word | We respond with Thanksgiving and partake in the Eucharist | We go forth to love and serve |

These four movements provide a framework for Paul's admonition, in 1 Cor. 14:40, "that all things should be done decently and in order" (NRSV). Christians in the Free Church and charismatic traditions may find liturgical worship over-structured. In response, Chan offers three considerations: First, additional Free-Church or charismatic types of services could be offered in addition to the primary liturgical worship service. Second, spontaneous charismatic expressions could have a place in liturgical worship services, as long as they are not disruptive or out of line. Finally, many essential elements, such as the laying on of hands, healing services, praying for the sick, and altar calls could be incorporated into formal liturgies.[54]

The nature of this study precludes a comprehensive study of the structure of the fourfold service; many other resources are available to assist one who is interested in liturgical worship practices.[55] A brief overview of each of the four parts is given below.

54. Ibid., 127.

55. Use of any Internet search engine will produce a myriad of

The Gathering reflects the beginning of a journey. One is leaving behind the daily routine of the world and entering a journey as a people of God. Orthodox Theologian Alexander Schmemann describes the theological implication of this initial element of liturgical worship: it is the time when the people are ". . . to be transformed into the Church of God."[56] During the Greeting, the service may include greeting, adoration, confession, and absolution.

As previously noted, the Proclamation of the Word is a sacramental event. If the liturgy follows the lectionary cycle, ". . . the sermon will truly be an exposition of the gospel, since the readings themselves are based on the gospel events set within the Christian calendar."[57] By using the lectionary cycle, emphasis is placed on the gospel story instead of the preacher because the pericope that will be the subject of the sermon is pre-selected by the Church, rather than by the preacher. During the second movement of the liturgy, the Proclamation of the Word, the service may include readings from the Old Testament, including the Psalms, or from the Epistles and the Gospels, as well as the Apostles' Creed or Nicene Creed, the prayers of the people (the intercessions), and the sign of peace.

Paul Brunner asserts that the celebration of the Eucharist was "an institutive act" performed by Jesus himself.[58] Chan explains:

---

liturgical resources. The following search terms may serve as a guide: "liturgical worship," "liturgical resources," "liturgica," "leiturgia" and "Lord's Supper."

56. Schmemann, *For the Life of the World*, 27.

57. Chan, *Liturgical Theology*, 134.

58. Brunner, *Worship in the Name of Jesus*, 162.

The rite of Holy Communion that the church observes is not a result of some historical event that
eventually produces a commemorative event.
It is not the creation of the community but the
creation of Jesus Christ himself. He instituted it
because he actualized or fulfilled the reality that
the bread and wine symbolize. He took ordinary
bread and wine and lifted them from ordinary
use after he prayed a prayer of thanksgiving. In
the same way, the words of institution and the
epiclesis in subsequent celebrations provide the
crucial link between ordinary bread and wine
and spiritual food and drink.[59]

The third movement of the service, the Eucharist,
includes the Offertory, the Great Thanksgiving, the Lord's
Prayer, the Breaking of Bread, Invitation, and Communion.
The fourth and last movement, the Dismissal, commemorates the ". . . sending out [of Christians] into the world
where the action of living and serving God is a continua-
tion of their worship."[60] The Dismissal may include a bene-
diction and a final "Sending Forth."

59. Chan, *Liturgical Theology*, 141.
60. Webber, *Blended Worship*, 46.

# Re-appropriating *Lex Orandi*:
# Six Practices for Congregations

## PRACTICE 1. RECOVER THE MYSTERY OF WORSHIP

CONTEMPORARY CHRISTIAN worship and preaching strives to be upbeat and relevant, offering a message with practical application. Yet one wonders if this practice has led to a generation of Christians who have lost all sense of the *mysterium tremendum* of worship, the overwhelming and awesome sense of the mystery of being in God's presence. Schmemann calls this ". . . the experience of the "Holy" . . . which is at the root of all religion."[1] More than any of the other three traditions discussed in this book, Orthodox Christians have maintained the sense that in liturgy one enters the presence of God with holy fear and trembling—keeping silent and experiencing a profound sense of holiness, mystery, reverence, and awe. "But the LORD is in His holy temple. Let all the earth keep silence before Him" (Hab 2:20 (NKJV)).

In *Worship Old and New*, Robert Webber explains that some Christians tend to define worship in two ways, neither

1. Schmemann, *Liturgy and Life*, 16.

of which grasps the imperative and mystery of worship. He writes:

> The first sees worship as *ascribing worth to God.* In this half truth definition the burden of worship is placed upon the worshipping community. The community of worship, it seems, must originate words and feelings or praise through music and prayer that God will find pleasing. The second is a *presentational approach to worship.* Here worship consists of packaged presentations to the "audience," so that they may hear the message. The error of both forms of worship is that they do not recognize the divine side of worship. In the divine side of worship, the God who has acted in history continues to act within the worshipping community in a saving and healing way as the community remembers, proclaims, enacts and celebrates with thanksgiving. That is to say that God, who is the object of worship, is also the subject of worship. As God's saving action is recalled and enacted, God is worshipped through the response of thanksgiving.[2]

And so, the first practice suggested here, in the service of recovering the mystery of worship, is this: Create a worship environment that invites people into a more "heavenly" aesthetic. From a religious education perspective, the aesthetics of the worship environment teaches important lessons about the theology of worship.

How can a congregation create a sacred space that expresses the glory of God and the feeling of heaven on earth? Many ideas come to mind: Use candles, icons, crosses, and chants. Sing songs from Taizé, simple verses gently re-

2. Webber, *Worship Old and New*, 262.

peated, over and again, which serve as a Christian mantra that penetrates the soul. Encourage people to light candles, gaze upon sacred images, and meditate silently. Until the medieval period, stained-glass windows were used not only to beautify the church, but also to illustrate the stories of the Bible and the holy tradition to people, almost all of whom were illiterate. In addition to the pulpit, add an altar/communion table and a baptismal font. "Free church people who have rejected the visual arts in worship are increasingly recognizing that the visual arts . . . assist us in praising God; and that the visual arts provide a form of witness."[3]

## PRACTICE 2. RECOVER AND DEVELOP A LITURGICAL WORSHIP SERVICE

Developing a liturgical worship service is advantageous to a contemporary Christian congregation in at least three ways: First, it reconnects the present-day church with the ancient church, whose practices many Christians express a desire to emulate. A worship service integrating both Word and Eucharist would satisfy this urge. In the mid-second century, just as or soon after the *Didache* was written, Justin Martyr describes a service as follows:

> And on the day called Sunday there is a meeting in one place of those who live in cities or the country, and the memoirs of the apostles or the writings of the prophets are read as long as time permits. When the reader has finished, the president in a discourse urges and invites [us] to the imitation of these noble things. Then we all stand up together and offer prayers. And, as said

3. Ibid., 211–212. See also Kennel, *Visual Arts and Worship*, 9.

before, when we have finished the prayer, bread is brought, and wine and water, and the president similarly sends up prayers and thanksgivings to the best of his ability, and the congregation assents, saying the Amen; the distribution, and reception of the consecrated [elements] by each one takes place and they are sent to the absent by the deacons.[4]

Second, liturgy seems to provide a fuller and richer worship experience. In addition to hearing the proclamation of God's Word, the community gathers around the Lord's Table to commemorate the life, death, and resurrection of Jesus Christ. In *Evangelicals on the Canterbury Trail*, Webber offers six suggestions as to why some Evangelicals might be attracted to the liturgical worship service: Because they (1) are seeking a return to mystery; (2) are longing for the experience of worship; (3) have a desire for sacramental reality; (4) are searching for spiritual identity; (5) wish to embrace the traditions of the whole church, and (6) want to develop a more holistic spirituality.[5]

Finally, the liturgical worship service will connect with people in the post-modern age more successfully than will any other form. The combination of Word and Eucharist integrates conceptual language with the symbolic language preferred by post-moderns. The congregation may thus move from being a passive community that listens to propositions towards being a participating community that listens to the Church's narrative and participates in the liturgy's signs and symbols.

4. Richardson, "The First Apology of Justin, the Martyr," 1.67.

5. Webber, *Evangelicals on the Canterbury Trail*, 21–85.

The two central acts of Christian worship are the Liturgy of the Word and the Liturgy of the Eucharist. In the mid-second century text, *The First Apology*, Justin Martyr provides a description of the two-part structure of worship followed by the early Christians. [6]

> This food we call Eucharist, of which no one is allowed to partake except one who believes that the things we teach are true, and has received the washing for forgiveness of sins and for rebirth, and who lives as Christ handed down to us. For we do not receive these things as common bread or common drink; but as Jesus Christ our Saviour being incarnate by God's word took flesh and blood for our salvation, so also we have been taught that the food consecrated by the word of prayer which comes from him, from which our flesh and blood are nourished by transformation, is the flesh and blood of that incarnate Jesus.
>
> For the apostles in the memoirs composed by them, which are called Gospels, thus handed down what was commanded them: that Jesus, taking bread and having given thanks, said, "Do this for my memorial, this is my body"; and likewise taking the cup and giving thanks he said, "This is my blood"; and gave it to them alone . . .
>
> And on the day called Sunday there is a meeting in one place of those who live in cities or the country, and the memoirs of the apostles or the writings of the prophets are read as long as time permits. When the reader has finished, the president in a discourse urges and invites [us] to the imitation of these noble things. Then we all stand

6. Webber, *Worship Old and New*, 54; See also Richardson, "The First Apology of Justin, the Martyr," Ch. 67, 287–88.

up together and offer prayers. And, as said before, when we have finished the prayer, bread is brought, and wine and water, and the president similarly sends up prayers and thanksgivings to the best of his ability, and the congregation assents, saying the Amen; the distribution, and reception of the consecrated [elements] by each one, takes place and they are sent to the absent by the deacons. Those who prosper, and who so wish, contribute, each one as much as he chooses to.[7]

Thus, the ancient structure of Christian worship is in two major parts: Word and Eucharist. Webber critiques the two popular expressions of worship mentioned above (the "ascribing worth to God" approach to worship and the "presentational" approach to worship) in many contemporary churches, as follows: "If worship is defined as ascribing worth to God, then worship, as in the case of many contemporary churches, consists of twenty or thirty minutes of singing songs *to* God, followed by teaching and ministry, neither of which is defined as worship. If worship is presentational, then the worship committee thinks in terms of a package of worship items that will be presented: music, drama, dance, sermon."[8]

Therefore, this two-part structure may serve as a model for contemporary worship.[9]

---

7. Richardson, "The First Apology of Justin, the Martyr," Ch. 66–67, 286–287.

8. Webber, *Worship Old and New*, 262.

9. For further study of early church worship, Webber, *Worship Old and New*; See also Webber, *Ancient-Future Worship*; See also Lake, "Didache."

| Liturgy of the Word |
| Readings from the prophets, apostles, and gospel |
| Sermon |
| Prayers of the People |

| Liturgy of the Eucharist |
| Presentation of bread, wine, and water |
| Eucharistic prayers read by presider |
| Amen response by the people |
| Distribution and reception of the consecrated elements (Deacons distribute elements to those absent) |
| Collection |

Historically, the Catholic Church and churches in the Anglican Communion have added two components to those outlined above: the acts of entrance and the acts of dismissal.

| FOUR MOVEMENTS OF WORSHIP | | | |
| The Liturgy of the Word | | The Liturgy of the Eucharist | |
| GATHERING | WORD | EUCHARIST | SENDING FORTH |
| We enter into God's presence | We hear God's Word | We re-spond with Thanksgiving and partake of the Eucharist | We go forth to love and serve |

The models described above can be used to help move churches away from "programmed" worship to "narrative" worship. "It [worship] assembles people into the Body of Christ . . . It narratives God's communication . . . in the service of the Word. It narrates a proper response of thanksgiving at the table of the Lord. It narrates the people's movement out of worship and into the world to love and serves the Lord."[10]

## PRACTICE 3. RECOVER OR INTRODUCE THE LITURGICAL/CHURCH YEAR

The liturgical year offers an organized and historically root-ed, Christ-centered rhythm to liturgical life, a rhythm that recalls the life, death, and resurrection of Jesus in a year-long cycle. The use of the structure of the liturgical year encourages both ". . . individual Christians and congrega-tions to practice Christian-year spirituality."[11] Protestants, generally, celebrate Christmas and Easter. While these two holidays are surely central days in the life of the Church, a fuller, richer, and more balanced Christian-year spirituality could be experienced by living out the liturgical year. As explained earlier, what unfolds over the course of the year is the ". . . whole mystery of Christ from his Incarnation and Nativity through his Ascension, to Pentecost and the expec-tation of the blessed hope of the coming of the Lord."[12] The chart below offers a brief overview of the liturgical year.

10. Webber, *Worship Old and New*, 263.

11. Webber, *Ancient-Future Time*, 15.

12. *CCC*, para. 1194.

| LITURGICAL YEAR[13] | | |
|---|---|---|
| **Season** | **Emphasis** | **Spiritual Challenge** |
| **Advent** *Four Sundays before Christmas Day* | Readiness for the coming of Christ at the end of history and at Bethlehem | To repent and be ready for the second coming of Christ. Allow an eager longing for the coming of the Messiah to be birthed in your heart |
| **Christmas** *December 25 to January 5* | The fulfillment of Israel's longing. The Messiah has come. The prophecies have been fulfilled. | Embrace an incarnational spirituality. Let Christ be born within you in a new way. |
| **Epiphany** *January 6* | The manifestation of Jesus to all as Savior not only for the Jews but for the whole world. | Make a new commitment to allow Jesus to be manifest in and through your life. |
| **Epiphany Season** (Also called Ordinary Time[14]) *After Epiphany January 6 to Lent* | A journey with Christ in his ministry as he manifests himself as the Son of God through signs and wonders. | Learn to manifest the life of Christ through the witness of life and deeds. |
| **Lent** *Ash Wednesday to Wednesday of Holy Week* | A time to travel with Jesus toward his death. | Lent is a time for repentance through self-examination and renewal through identification with the journey of Jesus. A time of prayer, fasting and almsgiving. |

13. Webber, *Ancient-Future Time*, 16.

14. Ordinary time does not mean common. Rather, it comes from the word "ordinal" which means "counted time." The weeks of ordinary time following Epiphany and Pentecost are numbered, e.g., the "First Sunday after Epiphany," the "Second Sunday after Pentecost," etc. See Bratcher, "Ordinary Time."

| Season | Emphasis | Spiritual Challenge |
|---|---|---|
| **The Great Triduum** *Maundy Thursday, Good Friday, Holy Saturday* | The most crucial time in the history of salvation. On Thursday, Jesus celebrates the Passover meal and washes the feet of the disciples. On Friday, Jesus is crucified. On Saturday, we rest and prepare for the Easter Vigil and Jesus' resurrection. | The three great days are a time of fasting and prayer. We commit to live in the pattern of Jesus' death and resurrection, the pattern of life into which we have been baptized. |
| **Easter** *Easter Sunday to Pentecost* | The celebration of Jesus' resurrection and salvation of the world. The most crucial event in the Church year. | Here is the source of the spiritual life. We are called to die to sin in the death of Christ and rise to the life of the Spirit in resurrection spirituality. |
| **Pentecost** *Pentecost Day to Advent* | The celebration of the birth of the Church with the coming of the Holy Spirit. | A time to celebrate the birth of the Church. |
| **Pentecost Season** (Also called Ordinary Time[15]) *After Pentecost* *From Pentecost to Advent* | After Pentecost, witnesses spread the gospel; recalls the growth and trials of the early church. | A time to embrace the teaching of the church and to go deeper into the truths of God's saving events in history. |

15. Bratcher, "Ordinary Time."

The Liturgical Year: A Cyclical View

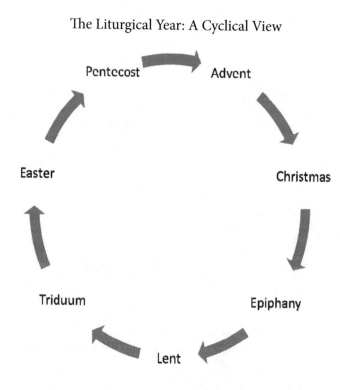

## PRACTICE 4. RECOVER AND IMPLEMENT A LECTIONARY CATECHESIS

As explained earlier, the readings for the Catholic liturgy follow a three-year lectionary cycle. Lectionaries have also become increasingly popular among Protestant denominations. The lectionary most commonly used in North America is the work of the Consultation on Common Texts, ". . . an ecumenical consultation of liturgical scholars and denominational representatives from the United States and

Canada, who produce liturgical texts for use in common by North American Christian Churches."[16]

The lectionary is divided into three, one-year cycles simply identified as Cycle A, Cycle B, and Cycle C. Cycle A focuses on the Gospel of Matthew; Cycle B focuses on the Gospel of Mark; and Cycle C focuses on the Gospel of Luke. The Gospel of John is used intentionally and intermittently throughout all three cycles, particularly through the Lenten and Easter seasons.

What is most significant about the use of the lectionary, pedagogically speaking, is the connection between worship and Christian education. The Bible passages for the Sunday liturgy may also serve as the biblical focus examined during that week's teaching lesson, thereby connecting the aim of the lesson with the theme of the worship service. This model provides a pedagogical/liturgical logic reinforcing the relationship between *lex credendi*, the learning aspect of the faith, and *lex orandi*, the worshipping aspect of the faith. Furthermore, by studying the same passages across all

16. The Consultation on Common Texts. The current membership of the CCT includes delegates from the following churches or agencies: Anglican Church of Canada, Canadian Conference of Catholic Bishops, Christian Church (Disciples of Christ), Christian Reformed Church in North America, Church of the Brethren, Episcopal Church, Evangelical Lutheran Church in America, Evangelical Lutheran Church in Canada, Free Methodist Church in Canada, Liturgy and Life: American Baptist Fellowship for Liturgical Renewal, Lutheran Church-Missouri Synod, Mennonite Church, National Conference of Catholic Bishops of the United States, Polish National Catholic Church, Presbyterian Church (U.S.A.), Presbyterian Church in Canada, Reformed Church in America, Unitarian Universalist Christian Fellowship, United Church of Canada, United Church of Christ, and United Methodist Church.

age groups and grades, common intergenerational learning is encouraged. The director of Christian education has the flexibility of using this model in Sunday school, small groups, or home churches. For example, small groups and house churches that meet on a weekly basis could use the Sunday Bible passages as the focus of study and discussion the week prior to or after its use during worship, further reinforcing the lessons learned there.[17]

| THE LECTIONARY | | | |
|---|---|---|---|
| Cycle Starting on the First Sunday of Advent | Cycle A | Cycle B | Cycle C |
| Gospel Focus | Gospel of Matthew | Gospel of Mark | Gospel of Luke |
| | John—used primarily in Lent | John—used primarily in Lent | John—used primarily in Lent |

Given the longstanding tradition, in many churches and among many Christians, of reading and studying the entire Bible in one year, perhaps the Orthodox Church's one-year lectionary cycle may be a more appropriate model than the three-year version. The annual cycle of gospel reading is generally structured (with some exceptions) as follows:

17. For information on the lectionary or for the schedule of readings, visit the following websites: *The Voice* (http://www.lectionary.org); *The Lectionary* (http://www.cresourcei.org/RCLmenu.html.); *The Text this Week* (http://www.textweek.com).

(1) The Gospel of John: Read from Easter (*Pascha*) until Pentecost Sunday (50 days after Easter).

(2) The Gospel of Matthew: Read from Pentecost to the Elevation of the Holy Cross (September 14).[18]

(3) The Gospel of Luke: Read from the Elevation of the Holy Cross (September 14) to Great Lent.[19]

(4) The Gospel of Mark: Read during the Lenten period.[20]

## PRACTICE 5. RECOVER THE LORD'S SUPPER AS THE OCCASION FOR ALTAR CALLS

The Altar Call is a tradition and remains standard practice in many Christian churches. It is an invitation to repent and "come forward" to "accept Christ" into one's heart. The Altar Call is a revival technique adopted by Charles Finney in the early nineteenth century. It was not used in the earlier "awakenings" of John Wesley, George Whitefield, or Jonathan Edwards, ". . . all of whom stressed the priority of and all-sufficiency of grace."[21]

"The invitation given after the sermon, if it is to be given at all, should be to profess Christ publicly on the part of those who have received him inwardly."[22] The Altar Call is an extra-biblical devotional tradition, one which Bloesch

18. From the twelfth week, it is read on Saturdays and Sundays while the Gospel of Mark is read on the remaining weekdays.

19. From the thirteenth week, it is only read on Saturdays and Sundays, while Mark's Gospel is read on the remaining weekdays.

20. Taken directly and only slightly modified from "Lectionary," http://orthodoxwiki.org/Lectionary.

21. Bloesch, *Essentials of Evangelical Theology*, Vol. 2, 95.

22. Ibid., 95.

supports: "We urge . . . that people be encouraged to sur-render to Christ and forsake their sins in the situation of preaching and hearing of the Word, for otherwise preaching is simply a preparation for an extrabiblical devotional practice viewed as the climax of the service."[23]

Holy Communion should generally be the occasion of dedication and surrender. When one is "convicted" of sin and thus moved to draw closer to Christ, the Eucharist serves as the sacramental medium for this union—the true Altar Call. As previously stated, only baptized Christians should normally partake of communion. If, however, someone who has not been baptized is consciously led to do so, this should be understood as the desire of a person seeking to know Christ more intimately. Bloesch suggests that the rise in popularity of the Altar Call may be due to ". . . the loss of the penitential and decision-character of the blessed sacrament."[24] At this point, a proper Christian initiation method in which a person begins a more formal Christian formation/discipleship process is appropriate.

## PRACTICE 6. RECOVER EVANGELICAL, CHRISTOCENTRIC PREACHING

As previously mentioned, from a pedagogical perspective, preaching is *the* primary form of *didache*, the teaching or religious education of God's people through the *kerygma*, the proclamation of the Word of God and evangelization of

23. Ibid., 102.
24. Ibid., 95.

the gospel. Recovering evangelical, Christocentric preaching is therefore imperative.[25]

## The Decline of Preaching

Augustine, Bernard of Clairvaux, Thomas Aquinas, Savonarola, and Vincent Ferrer are a few well-known, classical Catholic theologians noted for their evangelical biblical-expository preaching. In addition to these major figures, countless numbers of Christians have preached the gospel well and fully over the centuries. Yet there has been an overall general decline in both the value attached to—and the quality of much of—the preaching done in Christian churches. Three historical reasons for this decline are offered here: First, during the medieval period, the sacrifice of the liturgy was elevated above the preaching of the gospel. Second, biblical sermons were replaced by homiletic sermons, exhortations on moral themes, and ecclesial teachings. Finally, the rise of mysticism overtook the centrality of the preaching of Christ in salvation.[26] Comparing the content of the preaching of the early church with that of well-known medieval mystic and theologian, Meister Eckhart, Bloesch writes: "The mystics maintained that God acts without instrumentality and without ideas (Eckhart). Their aim was to ascend beyond the rational to an intuitive apprehension of God in himself. Preaching was simply an external aid by which one was drawn to focus attention on the supernatural and suprahistorical. In the New Testament

---

25. For a contemporary reflection on these five classic designations, see Harris, *Fashion Me a People*.

26. Bloesch, *Essentials of Evangelical Theology*, Vol. 2, 73.

church, the content of preaching was Christ crucified, risen and coming again. In the preaching of Meister Eckhart there was little about the events of salvation-history but much about the birth of Christ in the soul."[27]

It is interesting to note that the Catholic Church is currently seeking to recover its preaching ministry. *The Constitution of Sacred Liturgy*, a document written during the Second Vatican Council, affirms that "[t]he ministry of preaching is to be fulfilled most faithfully and carefully. The sermon, moreover, should draw its content mainly from scriptural and liturgical sources, for it is the proclamation of God's wonderful works in the history of salvation, which is the mystery of Christ ever made present and active in us."[28] A few years later, Pope Paul VI declared: "Preaching is the primary apostolate. Our ministry, Venerable Brethren, is before all else the ministry of the Word.[29] Protestantism, particularly in the Lutheran, Reformed, Puritan, and Pietist traditions, has historically maintained the importance of evangelical preaching. Evangelical preaching is intended to be a Christ-centered, biblical-expository message, empowered by the Holy Spirit; a message that convicts people of sin, provides an opportunity for repentance and conversion, and comforts people with redemption, the glorious gift of salvation and spiritual growth. Over the past two hundred years, under the impact of the work of Friedrich Schleiermacher the focus of Protestant preaching changed greatly. He emphasized the reality of one's experience of

27. Ibid., 73.

28. Abbott, *The Documents of Vatican Council II*, 149–150.

29. Cited in *The Reformed Journal*, Vol. 25, No. 6 (July–August 1975), 31.

God. About Schleiermacher, Bloesch writes: "The tenets of the Christian faith are only derivatives of the inner state of man. The Word is of secondary importance, for the divine is ineffable. What is of primary importance is not doctrinal fidelity but the cultivation of piety and religiousness. In his sermons Schleiermacher did not appeal to the Bible, but his aim was to not confront his hearers with the judgment and grace of a holy God but to awaken the God-consciousness within all people and to encourage moral effort."[30]

During the twentieth century, the great theologian Karl Barth was one who sought to recover evangelical, biblical preaching.[31] In his writing, he speaks of both the impossibility and necessity of preaching.[32] For Barth, the content of preaching should be ". . . the announcement of God's grace and judgment which has taken place on behalf of all humankind in Jesus Christ—in his incarnation, crucifixion and resurrection."[33] Barth believes that preaching does not offer salvation, but rather proclaims a finished work of salvation. That is, hearers receive an awareness of salvation that is already theirs. The preacher does not call people to a decision of salvation. The job of the preacher is to make known the conversion of all humankind that has already taken place in Jesus Christ.[34] Evangelical theologians find some of Barth's teaching problematic. According to Bloesch, Barth seems to understand preaching ". . . not as an instrument or agency of salvation but only as a testi-

30. Bloesch, *Essentials of Evangelical Theology*, Vol. 2, 78.
31. Karl Barth, *The Word of God.*
32. Ibid., 183–217.
33. Bloesch, *Essentials of Evangelical Theology*, Vol. 2, 79.
34. Ibid., 80.

mony to a salvation already completed."[35] It focuses on the past work of Christ, and not the present, ongoing work of Christ. Nevertheless, the resurgence of interest in the recovery of evangelical preaching and thinking owes a great debt to Barth.

Dietrich Bonhoeffer, another great twentieth-century Protestant theologian popular with Evangelicals, was greatly influenced by Karl Barth, with whom he studied. According to one of his biographers, Bonhoeffer believed that, ". . . the word of the sermons has, and is, the presence of Christ."[36] Bonhoeffer himself writes: "Nothing is more concrete than the real voice of Christ speaking in the sermon."[37] He emphasizes the eternal consequences of preaching the gospel when he asserts that ". . . He has put His Word in our mouth. He wants it to be spoken through us. If we hinder His Word, the blood of the sinning brother will be upon us. If we carry out His Word, God will save our brother through us."[38]

Bonhoeffer maintains that there is a time for the church to speak and a time for the church to be silent. "The church should remain silent when it has so falsified its message that it is compromised before the world."[39] According to Bonhoeffer, Bloesch writes, ". . . the secularization of faith [has] made it supremely difficult to proclaim the Word of faith in its purity and power and . . . therefore the church should seek to witness simply by Christian presence . . . He envisioned a period of silence and struggle, but in the end it

35. Ibid., 80.

36. Bonhoeffer, *Letters and Papers from Prison*, xiii.

37. Bethge, *Dietrich Bonhoeffer*, 361.

38. Bonhoeffer, *Life Together*, 108.

39. Bonhoeffer, *The Cost of Discipleship*, 188.

would once again be the proclaimed Word that would renew the Church. When the Word is proclaimed again, however, it will be a dereligionized Word, a Word liberated from its captivity to a religio-cultural tradition of the past."[40]

Recognizing that this German-born, Lutheran pastor-theologian was writing within the context of, and in response to, the atrocities of Nazi Germany that ultimately took his life, Evangelical theologians nevertheless have two problems with Bonhoeffer's teaching, just as they do with Barth's. As Bloesch suggests, instead of silence or refraining from direct proclamation in the face of secularization, perhaps it is precisely at this time ". . . when the message needs to be uttered by those who have been granted spiritual and theological discernment."[41] Second, while the use of new imagery is certainly helpful in clarifying and illuminating biblical concepts, it is the rich biblical language which reconnects with sacramental faith and with the early church traditions.[42]

## Preaching the Good News and the Bad News

Evangelical preaching proclaims ". . . the whole counsel of God and this includes the Law of God as well as the Gospel, sin as well as salvation, hell as well as heaven."[43] The notion here is to avoid both a condemning word which does not offer hope for redemption and a positive message that fails to address the reality of sin and humanity's fallen nature,

40. Bloesch, *Essentials of Evangelical Theology*, Vol. 2, 81, 82.
41. Ibid., 82.
42. Ibid., 83.
43. Ibid., 83.

for neither reflects an authentic gospel message. Bloesch explains: "We must preach not only the good news of God's mercy and love but also the bad news of his wrath and judgment on sin . . . The Gospel is not only an announcement of unfathomable grace but an invitation to surrender in faith and repentance."[44] This is seen in Acts 20:25–27 where, in typically direct fashion, Paul says farewell to the Ephesians: "And now I know that none of you, among whom I have gone about proclaiming the kingdom, will ever see my face again. Therefore I declare to you this day that I am not responsible for the blood of any of you, for I did not shrink from declaring to you the whole purpose of God" (NRSV).

The purpose of evangelical preaching is to proclaim the gospel message so that a person may experience a new freedom, a liberation, which will enable him or her to repent from sin and embrace the grace and mercy of Jesus Christ.[45] In the following excerpt from his writing, Bloesch describes the classic understanding of the process of evangelical preaching which leads to decision-making:

> The hearer can make a decision for Christ, though not on the basis of his own power or wisdom. The Holy Spirit is poured out on all who hear the good news of what God has done for us in Christ, but the Spirit can be quenched and grieved by those who taste of its power and then reject the Gospel. Those who hear the Gospel and refuse to heed its call damn themselves, for they had the opportunity but squandered it. If they accept, of course, the credit goes to the grace of

44. Ibid., 83–84.
45. Ibid., 84.

> God, since it was the Spirit who enabled them
> to accept. On the other hand, if they refuse, the
> blame is on them, since their hardness of heart
> did not allow the Spirit to have full sway in their
> lives. Therefore, the Gospel is to one a "fragrance
> from death to death" but to another a "fragrance
> from life to life." (2 Cor. 2:26, NRSV)[46]

Preaching the law of God and the gospel in an evangelical way focuses particularly on the understanding of three elements: First, the law of God is used as a mirror to highlight the sin of humanity. Second, the gospel presents the gift of grace found in Jesus Christ. Finally, if and when a person accepts the gospel message, the law of God then becomes a guide to Christian living.

## The Nature of Evangelical Preaching

Evangelical preaching avoids cultural preaching. Evangelical preaching is biblical as opposed to sectarian. Cultural preaching tends to focus on sanctification over justification, i.e., how to live a Christian life without the challenge to repentance, conversion, and surrender to Christ. Evangelical preaching focuses on both. Using the term coined by Bonhoeffer, Evangelicals would consider cultural preaching "cheap grace," which Bonhoeffer explains as follows:

> Cheap grace is the preaching of forgiveness
> without requiring repentance, baptism without
> church discipline, Communion without confession, absolution without personal confession.
> Cheap grace is grace without discipleship, grace

46. Ibid., 84.

without the cross, grace without Jesus Christ, living and incarnate . . . Such grace is costly because it calls us to follow, and it is grace because it calls us to follow Jesus Christ. It is costly because it costs a man his life, and it is grace because it gives a man the only true life. It is costly because it condemns sin and grace because it justifies the sinner. Above all, it is costly because it cost the life of his Son: "ye were bought with a price," and what has cost God much cannot be cheap for us. Above all it is grace because God did not reckon his Son too dear a price to pay for our life, but delivered him up for us. Costly grace is the Incarnation of God.[47]

Evangelical preaching does not neglect religious experiences. But it is also faithful to proper biblical doctrine. Evangelical preaching proclaims Christ, not theology; yet it must be theologically sound. It should focus on the Word of God, and not on the word or personality of the preacher.[48]

One currently popular type of preaching is interactive or dialogue preaching. One form of it occurs when two ministers share their opinion on the same issue; another form involves the minister interacting with the congregation. While this kind of interaction may be appropriate for small-group gatherings or catechetical, formation settings, it is not faithful to the classical form of evangelical preaching, as Bloesch argues: "Dialogue preaching signifies an evasion of our prophetic mandate. It also indicates an abdication of evangelical preaching, since the focus is on

47. Bonhoeffer, *The Cost of Discipleship*, 44–45.
48. Bloesch, *Essentials of Evangelical Theology*, Vol. 2, 93.

seeking the truth in openness rather than proclaiming it with conviction. The real dialogue should be between Jesus Christ and the worshipper—Christ speaking through the preacher and the Scripture and man responding in prayers and hymns or praise.[49]

On the one hand, cultural preaching is also an evasion of the prophetic mandate, for it often hides behind political correctness and societal niceties instead of preaching with authority and standing boldly on the Word of God. On the other hand, "condemning" preaching is counter-prophetic as well, for it tends to put people down instead of building people up.

Evangelical preaching should be kerygmatic rather than apologetic. The preacher stands on the authority of sacred Scripture and is emboldened by the Holy Spirit. Evangelical preaching does not need to defend the validity of the claims of the Christian faith; instead it proclaims the Good News, the "Great Narrative" of Jesus Christ.[50]

Kerygmatic preaching is not based on current events but on the scriptural message. According to Bloesch, "Kerygmatic preaching is sacramental rather than ethical because through this preaching sins are forgiven and hearts and minds transformed."[51]

True Evangelical preaching is evangelical (biblical) rather than moralistic. "This means the fidelity to the Word of God is more important than an appeal to the understanding or emotions of our hearers."[52] Evangelical preaching is

49. Ibid., 97.
50. Ibid., 94.
51. Ibid., 95.
52. Ibid., 95.

charismatic in the sense that the preacher should be led by the Holy Spirit. Charismatic preaching does not necessarily have to display enthusiastic emotion. While prepared to preach, the preacher relies on the Holy Spirit rather than on his or her own resources and wisdom.[53] Finally, evangelical preaching is socially prophetic. That is, it addresses sins that have infiltrated society as well as issues of social injustice.[54]

53. Ibid., 96.
54. Ibid., 97.

# Bibliography

*Catechism of the Catholic Church*, 2nd ed. Washington, DC: United States Conference of Catholic Bishops, 1994, 1997.

———. "Church Year," from the Orthodox Church of America. No pages. Online: http://www.oca.org/OCchapter.asp?SID=2&ID=64

———. "Deification." In *The Orthodox Study Bible: Ancient Christianity Speaks to Today's World*. Nashville, TN: Thomas Nelson, 2008.

———. "Didache." In *The Apostolic Fathers*, Vol. 1, LCL. Edited by Kirsopp Lake. Cambridge, MA: Harvard University Press, 1998.

———. "The Acts of the Apostles." In *The Holy Bible: The New Oxford Annotated Bible with the Apocryphal/Deuterocanonical Books, New Revised Standard Version*. Edited by Bruce M. Metzger and Roland E. Murphy. New York: Oxford University Press, 1991.

———. "The Lectionary." In *The Voice: Biblical and Theological Resources for Growing Christians*, 2007. Online: http://www.cresourcei.org/RCLmenu.html. In *The Lectionary*. Online: http://www.lectionary.org. In *The Text This Week*. Online: http://www.textweek.com. In *Orthodox Wiki, 2010*. http://orthodoxwiki.org/Lectionary.

———. "The Teaching of the Twelve Apostles." In Christian Classics Ethereal Library. No pages. Online: http://www.ccel.org/ccel/schaff/anf07.viii.html.

Abbott, Walter M. ed., *The Documents of Vatican Council II*. New York: American Press, 1966.

Babin, Pierre. *The New Era in Religious Communication*. Minneapolis, MN: Fortress, 1991.

Barth, Karl. *The Word of God and the Word of Man*. Translated by Douglas Horton. New York: Harper & Row, 1957.

Bethge, Eberhard. *Dietrich Bonhoeffer*. Minneapolis, MN: Augsburg, 2000.

Bloesch, Donald G. *Essentials of Evangelical Theology*, 2 vols. Peabody, MA: Hendrickson, 1978, 2006.

Bonhoeffer, Dietrich. *Letters and Papers from Prison*. New York: Simon & Schuster, 1953, 1997.

———. *Life Together*. New York: Harper Collins, 1954, 1978.

———. *The Cost of Discipleship*. New York: Simon & Schuster, 1959, 1995.

Bratcher, Dennis. "Ordinary Time: Counted Time of the Church Year." In *The Voice: Biblical and Theological Resources for Growing Christians*, 2007. No pages. Online: http://www.cresourcei.org/cyordinary.html.

Brown, Raymond E., Joseph A. Fitzmyer, and Roland E. Murphy. *The New Jerome Biblical Commentary*. Englewood Cliffs: Prentice Hall, 1968, 1990.

Brunner, Peter. *Worship in the Name of Jesus*. Translated by M. H. Bertram. Minneapolis, MN: Fortress, 1993.

Calvin, John. *Commentary on the Epistles of Paul the Apostle to the Corinthians*, II, 5, 19. Translated by John Pringle. Edinburgh: Calvin Translation Society, 1849.

Chan, Simon. *Liturgical Theology: The Church as Worshiping Community*. Downers Grove, IL: InterVarsity, 2006.

Clendenin, Daniel B. *Eastern Orthodox Christianity: A Western Perspective*. Grand Rapids, MI: Baker, 1994.

———. *Eastern Orthodox Theology: A Contemporary Reader*. Grand Rapids, MI: Baker, 1995, 2003.

De Letter, P. *Prosper of Aquitaine: Defense of St. Augustine*. Westminster: Newman Press, 1963.

Dillon, Richard J. "Acts of the Apostles." In *The New Jerome Biblical Commentary*. Edited by Raymond E. Brown, Joseph A. Fitzmyer, and Roland E. Murphy. Englewood Cliffs, NJ: Prentice Hall, 1968, 1990.

Erickson, Millard J. *Introducing Christian Doctrine*, 2nd ed. Grand Rapids, MI: Baker, 2001.

———. *Christian Theology*, 2nd ed. Grand Rapids, MI: Baker, 1983, 1984, 1985, 1998.

Forsyth, P. T. *Congregationalism and Reunion*. London: Independent Press, 1952.

Geisler, Norman. "Avoid All Contradictions: A Surrejoinder to John Dahms," *Journal of the Evangelical Theological Society* 22:2, June 1979.

——— and Ralph E. MacKenzie. *Roman Catholics and Evangelicals: Agreements and Differences.* Grand Rapids, MI: Baker, 1995.

Grenz, Stanley J. *Theology for the Community of God.* Grand Rapids, MI: Eerdmans, 2000.

Grudem, Wayne A. *Systematic Theology: An Introduction to Biblical Doctrine.* Grand Rapids, MI: Eerdmans, 1994.

Harris, Maria. *Fashion Me a People: Curriculum in the Church.* Louisville. KY: Westminster John Knox, 1989.

Hauck, A. "Prosper of Aquitaine." In *Petri-Reuchlin*, Volume IX of the *New Schaff-Herzog Encyclopedia of Religious Knowledge.* Edited by Philip Schaff; Grand Rapids, MI: Christian Classics Ethereal Library, 1953, 2003.

Hawking, Stephen W. *A Brief History of Time.* New York: Bantam Books, 1988, 1998.

Heron, Alasdair I. C. *Table and Tradition.* Philadelphia: Westminster John Knox, 1984.

Hohenstein, Charles R. "Lex Orandi, Lex Credendi: Cautionary Notes." *Wesleyan Theological Journal* 32:2 (1997), 140–157. Online: http://wesley.nnu.edu/sermons-essays-books/wesleyan-theological-journal-1966-2009/.

Hopko, Thomas. *The Orthodox Church: Worship*, Vol. 2 of *The Orthodox Faith.* Syosset, NY: The Orthodox Church in America, 1997.

Kelly, J. N. D. *Early Christian Doctrines.* New York: Harper & Row, 1960.

Kennel, LeRoy. *Visual Arts and Worship.* Worship Series No. 14. Newton, KS: Faith and Life Press, 1983.

Kuhn, Thomas S. *The Structure of Scientific Revolutions.* Chicago: University of Chicago Press, 1962, 1996.

Lake, Kirsopp. "Didache: The Teaching of the Twelve Apostles." In *The Apostolic Fathers*, Vol. 1. Cambridge, MA: Harvard University Press, 1912, 1914, 1919, 1925, 1930, 1946, 1949, 1952, 1959, 1965, 1970, 1975, 1977, 1985, 1998.

Lossky, Vladimir. *The Mystical Theology of the Eastern Church.* Crestwood, NY: St. Vladimir's Seminary Press, 1944, 1976.

———. *Orthodox Theology: An Introduction.* Crestwood, NY: St. Vladimir's Press, 1978.

———. "The Procession of the Holy Spirit in Orthodox Trinitarian Theology." In Daniel B.

Clendenin, *Eastern Orthodox Theology: A Contemporary Reader.* Grand Rapids: Baker, 1995, 2003.

Luther, Martin. *D. Martin Luther's Werke.* Weimarer: H. Böhlau, 1883.

Meyendorff, John. *Byzantine Theology: Historical Trends and Doctrinal Themes.* New York: Fordham University Press, 1974, 1979.

Miller, Randolph Crump. *Theologies of Religious Education.* Birmingham, AL: Religious Education Press, 1995.

Oden, Thomas C. *Life in the Spirit.* Vol. 3 of *Systematic Theology.* San Francisco: Harper & Row, 1992.

Patsavos, Lewis J. "Dating Pascha in the Orthodox Church." No pages. Online: http://lent.goarch.org/articles/lent_dating_pascha.asp.

———. "The Calendar of the Orthodox Church." No pages. Online: http://www.goarch.org/ourfaith/ourfaith7070.

Pope Paul VI. "*Ecclesiam Suam*, Encyclical of Pope Paul VI on the Church, Vatican: Rome, 1964. Online: http://www.vatican.va/holy_father/paul_vi/encyclicals/documents/hf_p-vi_enc_06081964_ecclesiam_en.html

Richardson, Cyril C. "The Teaching of the Twelve Apostles, Commonly Called the Didache." In *Early Christian Fathers*, Vol. 1. Philadelphia: Westminster, 1953. Online: http://www.ccel.org/ccel/schaff/anf07.viii.html.

———. "The First Apology of Justin, the Martyr." In *Early Christian Fathers*, Vol. 1. Philadelphia: Westminster, 1953. Online: http://www.ccel.org/ccel/richardson/fathers.x.ii.html?highlight=justin,martyr#highlight.

Schmemann, Alexander. *Introduction to Liturgical Theology.* Crestwood, NY: St. Vladimir's Seminary Press, 1966, 2003.

———. *Liturgy and Life: Christian Development through Liturgical Experience.* New York: Orthodox Church in America, 1974.

———. *For the Life of the World: Sacraments and Orthodoxy.* Crestwood, NY: St. Vladimir's Seminary Press, 1973.

Sokolof, Archpriest Dimitrii. *A Manual of the Orthodox Church's Divine Services*. 3rd ed. Jordanville, NY: Holy Trinity Monastery, 2001.

Taft, Robert F. *The Byzantine Rite: A Short History*. Collegeville, MN: The Liturgical Press, 1992.

Tarasar, Constance J. "Orthodox Theology and Religious Education." In Randolph Crump Miller, *Theologies of Religious Education*. Birmingham, AL: Religious Education Press, 1995.

Tyneh, Carl S. *Orthodox Christianity: Overview and Bibliography*. Hauppauge, NY: Nova Science Publishers, 2003.

Van Slyke, Daniel G. "*Lex orandi lex credendi*: Liturgy as *Locus Theologicus* in the Fifth Century?" *Josephinum Journal of Theology* 11, No. 2 (Summer/Fall 2004): 130–151. Online: http://www.pcj.edu/journal/essays/vanslyke11-2.htm.

Ware, Timothy (Kallistos). *The Orthodox Church*. New York, NY: Penguin 1963, 1997.

———. "The Earthly Heaven," in Daniel B. Clendenin, *Eastern Orthodox Theology: A Contemporary Reader*. Grand Rapids, MI: Baker, 1995, 2003.

Webber, Robert E. "Agenda for the Church 1976–2000." In *Eternity*, Vol. 27, No. 1 (January 1976).

———. *Evangelicals on the Canterbury Trail*. Harrisburg, PA: Morehouse, 1989.

———. *Worship Old and New*, Rev. ed. Grand Rapids, MI: Zondervan, 1994.

———. *Blended Worship: Achieving Substance and Relevance in Worship*. Peabody, MA: Hendrickson, 1994, 2000.

———. *Ancient-Future Faith: Rethinking Evangelicalism for a Postmodern World*. Grand Rapids, MI: Baker, 1999.

———. *Ancient-Future Evangelism: Making your Church a Faith Forming Community*. Grand Rapids, MI: Baker, 2003.

———. *Ancient-Future Time: Forming Spirituality through the Christian Year*. Grand Rapids, MI: Baker, 2004.

———. *Ancient-Future Worship: Proclaiming and Enacting God's Narrative*. Grand Rapids, MI: Baker, 2008.

# DATE DUE